Reasoning with Democratic Values

ETHICAL PROBLEMS IN UNITED STATES HISTORY

Volume 1: 1607-1876

Reasoning
with Democratic Values

ETHICAL PROBLEMS
IN UNITED STATES HISTORY

Volume 1: 1607-1876

Alan L. Lockwood
University of Wisconsin
Madison, Wisconsin

David E. Harris
Oakland Schools
Pontiac, Michigan

TEACHERS
COLLEGE
PRESS

Teachers College, Columbia University
New York and London

Published by Teachers College Press, 1234 Amsterdam Avenue, New York, N.Y. 10027

Library of Congress Cataloging in Publication Data

Lockwood, Alan L., 1941–
    Reasoning with democratic values.

    Includes bibliographies.
    Contents: v. 1. 1607–1876 — v. 2. 1877 to the present.
    1. United States—History. 2. Decision-making (Ethics) [1. United States—History. 2. Decision making] I. Harris, David E., 1945–   II. Title.
    E178.1.L82 1985   973   84-8597
    ISBN 0-8077-6094-3 (v. 1)
    ISBN 0-8077-6095-1 (v. 2)

Grateful acknowledgment is made for permission to reprint the following material:

Excerpts (in "Madness in Massachusetts") from THE CRUCIBLE by Arthur Miller. Copyright © 1953, renewed 1981 by Arthur Miller. Reprinted by permission of Viking Penguin Inc.

Excerpts (in "A Luxury We Can't Afford") from 1776 by Peter Stone and Sherman Edwards. Copyright © 1969 by Peter Stone, © 1964 by Sherman Edwards. Reprinted by permission of Viking Penguin Inc.

Excerpt (in "Tears of Blood") from ROBERT E. LEE by John Drinkwater. Copyright © 1923, by Houghton Mifflin Company. Copyright © 1951 by Dairy Kennedy Drinkwater. Reprinted by permission of Houghton Mifflin Company.

Cover photo credits: Top right, bottom right, and bottom left (courtesy of the Library of Congress); middle (courtesy of the Massachusetts Historical Society); top left (courtesy of the State Historical Society of Wisconsin).

Manufactured in the United States of America

11 10 09 08 07   19 18 17 16 15 14 13

Contents

Dear Students,

This book is to accompany your study of United States history. We have written true stories showing people making difficult decisions. These decisions involved such basic values as authority, equality, liberty, life, loyalty, promise-keeping, property, and truth. We invite you to follow the stories of these decisions and make judgments about them.

In this volume there are 21 stories. Each story brings you in contact with an ethical problem from our history. For example, you will glimpse the tensions and fears of witchcraft in Salem, Massachusetts, during the 1690s. You will witness Thomas Jefferson's struggle with slavery. You will see Osceola resist removal of the Seminoles from Florida. You will be a bystander as Henry David Thoreau protests the Mexican War. You will follow Peter Still's efforts to free himself from slavery. You will observe Robert E. Lee make a fateful decision at the outbreak of the Civil War.

Although these events took place long ago, the values involved continue to influence our lives. We believe that citizens of today must often make decisions involving these values. That is why we have written this book.

Rational, intelligent citizens need to recognize value problems and think carefully about them. Therefore, we have presented you with questions and activities which, with your teacher's help, will allow you to do such thinking. We also think the stories will help you gain a deeper understanding of our nation's remarkable history.

We hope you find the stories interesting and our questions thought-provoking.

Alan L. Lockwood and David E. Harris

PART 1

The Colonial Era
(1607–1776)

Friends and Enemies

MARY DYER

Mary Dyer Led to Execution

The search for religious freedom was one reason that some colonists came to America. This was true of the Puritans who began settling in Massachusetts in the 1630s.

The Puritans objected to the Church of England. They wanted to "purify" the Church of England by ridding it of its rituals, the special clothing worn by the clergy, and other features they disliked.

In England, the Puritans had not been free to practice their religion without penalty. They were insulted, jailed, and sometimes beaten because their beliefs were unpopular. Finally they received permission to set up a colony in New England.

In Massachusetts the Puritans intended to set up a society based on their religious beliefs. Many of them hoped their system would become a model for others to follow. People who opposed or questioned the Puritan religion were seen as a threat to their ideal society and not permitted to stay in Massachusetts. Roger Williams, for example, had to leave Massachusetts. He later founded the colony of Rhode Island. Anne Hutchinson was sent from the colony because she questioned some of the teachings of the Puritan ministers.

Anne Hutchinson was expelled in 1635. At the meeting in which the officials formally sent Anne away, a young woman named Mary Dyer rose, took her hand, and walked from the building with her. The officials and others were shocked at Mary's defiance of authority.

Mary and her husband William were forced to leave Massachusetts. They went to Rhode Island where there was greater religious freedom. William held a number of important jobs there and eventually became attorney general of the colony.

In 1652, Mary and William accompanied Roger Williams on a business trip to London. When business was completed, William returned to Rhode Island, but Mary stayed in London for a few more years.

In England, Mary became a convert to the new religion of the Society of Friends, also known as the Quakers. Her new religious beliefs would eventually lead to a dramatic and tragic encounter with the Puritans in Massachusetts.

Puritan leaders despised the Quakers. For one thing, the Quakers believed in an idea called the *Inward Light*. According to this belief, God's will was written in the hearts of all people. If people sincerely examined their consciences, they could discover the true wishes of God. The Puritans did not accept this idea. They believed that ministers had to interpret the Bible and explain God's will to the people. Not just anyone could discover God's truth. This difference in belief was at the heart of the growing conflict between the Quakers and the Puritans.

Because each Quaker's conscience could reveal the word of God, obedience to conscience was more important than obedience to society's laws. If the laws of society conflicted with a person's conscience, then that person was to follow his or her conscience rather than the law. For the Puritans, the ministers determined God's will and, therefore, their rulings were the ones that the people were obliged to obey.

Puritan leaders feared that the Quaker beliefs would disrupt the order and purpose of the Massachusetts colony. The leaders also felt the Quakers would undermine proper religious authority. These seemed like genuine possibilities because many Quakers were eager to spread their beliefs and gain converts to the Society of Friends.

In October 1656, the Massachusetts General Court passed its first anti-Quaker law. According to this law, Quakers entering Massachusetts were to be whipped and jailed until they could be sent away. Any ship's captain who brought in Quakers would be fined 100 pounds. Finally, Massachusetts citizens who helped the Quakers would also be fined.

In July 1657, Mary Dyer and Ann Burdern, both Quakers, arrived in Boston. Mary was on her way back to her husband in Rhode Island. Neither woman had heard about the new law. Because of this they were not whipped. Ann was sent from the colony and Mary placed in jail until her husband could come for her. Before Mary was set free, William had to promise he would take her directly to Rhode Island and not permit her to speak to people along the way. William made the promise and they returned to Rhode Island.

In spite of the law and the brutal whippings, some Quakers continued to come to Massachusetts to spread their beliefs. In 1657 a tougher law was passed. According to this law, any male Quaker who returned to Massachusetts a second time would have his right ear cut off. If he returned a third time a hole would be burned through his tongue. Women Quakers were to be whipped but, after the third offense, they would be treated like the men.

In the following months, three Quaker men lost their right ears. One man, William Brend, was given 117 lashes with a thick rope that had been soaked in tar. Many Massachusetts residents were shocked by these mutilations, and some offered help to the Quakers. Nonetheless, an even stricter law was passed—but just barely. By a vote of 13 to 12, the General Court decided that Quakers who returned to Massachusetts after being banished would receive the death penalty.

The Puritan leaders believed it necessary to defend the new law, because many people thought it was too harsh. In defending the law the Puritan leaders made two points. First, they said the Quaker religion was incorrect and violated the central beliefs of Puritanism. Second, they said the death penalty was a form of self-defense. They said that Massachusetts residents were like a family and the colony was their house. If anyone broke into a house to do harm he or she could be killed in self-defense. In their words, "And if such person shall offer to intrude into the man's house amongst his children and servants, can any doubt but that in such a case the father of the family, if otherwise he cannot keep them out, may kill them?" The Puritan leaders believed that they had the right to decide who could enter the colony and, in the case of the Quakers, that they had made all possible efforts to keep them out. Thus was the death penalty justified.

Some Quakers, moved by the Inward Light, were not deterred by the new law. Mary Dyer and others came back into Massachusetts to protest the law. Not only did they believe the law was unjust, but also they said that, as British citizens, they had the right to travel freely through the colonies. The Puritan leaders did not agree, and Governor Endicott sentenced Mary and the two men, Marmaduke Stephenson and William Robinson, "to be hanged on the gallows till you are dead."

On October 27, 1659, Mary and the men were led to the hanging tree on Boston Commons. Mary watched as first William and then Marmaduke climbed the ladder and were hanged. Mary was next. She was blindfolded and made to climb the ladder. The noose was placed around her neck. There was a pause. The executioner did not kick away the ladder. Mary was brought down from the ladder and told she would not be hanged if she returned to Rhode Island within 48 hours.

The authorities had decided days before she was led to the tree that she would not be hanged. Governors from two other colonies had written protests and one of Mary's sons had begged she be set free.

She had been taken to the gallows to give her a frightful warning. Mary objected to being singled out, but she was put on a horse and returned to Rhode Island.

Over the winter Mary thought deeply about what had happened. She had probably been set free to calm public opinion against the hangings. As she thought about it she became even more convinced that the laws against Quakers were wrong. In the spring, apparently without discussing it with her family, she returned to Massachusetts.

In May 1660, she was again sentenced to die. She said to the governor: "I came in obedience to the will of God . . . desiring you to repeal your righteous laws of banishment on pain of death." The officials would not change the law.

Her husband, who was not a Quaker, begged the governor to set her free. In his letter he said she had returned secretly to Massachusetts without his consent. He wrote passionately: "I only say that yourselves have been and are or may be husbands to wife or wives, so am I, yea to one most dearly beloved: Oh do not deprive me of her." He was not to have his way.

On May 31, 1660, Mary was again taken to the hanging tree. Captain Webb, commander of the military guard, told her she was responsible for her own death because she knowingly broke the law. Mary replied that she was trying only to get an unjust law repealed.

Once again on the ladder Mary was told she would be set free if she promised to return to Rhode Island. Mary refused the offer and, this time, the ladder was kicked away.

King Charles opposed the hangings. He ordered that anyone accused of a crime which led to the death penalty would have to be sent to England for trial. In response to the King's order and increasing public resentment, the Puritans repealed the hanging law.

The major sources for this story were:

Hodges, George. *The Apprenticeship of Washington and Other Sketches of Significant Colonial Personages*. New York: Moffat, Yard, 1909.

Rogers, Horatio. *Mary Dyer of Rhode Island: The Quaker Martyr*. Providence: Preston and Rounds, 1896.

Smith, Don. "Mary Dyer: Conscientious Dissenter." *Annual Editions Readings in American History*. Guilford, Conn.: Duskin Publishing Group, 1972, pp. 50–57.

ACTIVITIES FOR "FRIENDS AND ENEMIES"

Write all answers on a separate sheet of paper.

Historical Understanding

Answer briefly:

1. Why did the Puritans come to Massachusetts? What did they want to accomplish?

2. What did religious freedom mean to the Puritans?

3. What was the idea of the *Inward Light*? How did it conflict with Puritan belief?

Reviewing the Facts of the Case

Answer briefly:

1. What were the provisions of the first anti-Quaker law? The second?

2. How did the Puritan leaders justify the death penalty? Why did they feel it was necessary to write a justification?

3. Why did Mary and other Quakers go to Massachusetts in spite of the laws that had been passed? What happened to Mary after she received her first death sentence?

4. What did Captain Webb say to Mary before she died? How did she reply?

5. How did King Charles react to the hanging law?

Analyzing Ethical Issues

In this story there are a number of incidents involving the following values:

AUTHORITY: a value concerning what rules or people should be obeyed and the consequences for disobedience.

LIBERTY: a value concerning what freedoms people should have
and the limits that may be justifiably placed upon those
freedoms.

LIFE: a value concerning when, if ever, it is justifiable to threaten
or take a life.

In some incidents these values were in conflict and a decision was
made to choose one over another.

For example:

DECISION	VALUE IN CONFLICT	VALUE CHOSEN
Mary returned to Massachusetts after being warned.	*Her liberty versus Puritan authority.*	*She chose her liberty.*

Find another incident in which two values were in conflict and a
decision was made to choose one over the other. Following the above
example, write out the decision, the value in conflict, and the value
chosen.

Expressing Your Reasoning

1. Mary Dyer had many warnings not to return to Massachusetts.
   Should she have returned? Why or why not?

2. Were the Puritans right in passing the first anti-Quaker law? Why
   or why not? When the Quakers kept returning, were the Puritan
   leaders right in passing harsher laws? Why or why not?

3. When the death penalty was passed, a self-defense argument was
   written as part of the justification. If you believe it was wrong to
   pass the death penalty against the returning Quakers, write a paragraph explaining why the self-defense argument was not a good
   justification. If you believe they were right in passing the death
   penalty, write a paragraph explaining why you agree with their
   decision.

4. Captain Webb said that Mary was responsible for her own death
   because she knew she was breaking the law. Do you agree with
   Webb? Why or why not?

5. *Seeking Additional Information.* In making decisions about such

questions as those above, we often feel we need more information before we are satisfied with our judgment. Choose one of the above questions about which you would want more information than is presented in the story. What additional information would you like? Why would that information help you make a more satisfactory decision?

Madness in Massachusetts

SALEM WITCH TRIALS

(*Courtesy of the Library of Congress*)

The Witch Number 1

The hardships faced by the colonists are difficult for us to imagine today. Severe weather, difficulties in land cultivation, Indian attacks, and disease made survival from one year to the next an achievement. The first English attempt to establish a colony in Virginia was a complete failure. When supply ships arrived at Roanoke in 1591, not a single survivor could be found. The Jamestown colony, settled in 1607, managed to endure, but after the first six months about half of the original 120 settlers had died.

Many of the Jamestown settlers were interested in finding gold and less interested in staying in the colony. This was not true of the settlers in Massachusetts. Both the Pilgrims and the Puritans intended to make a home in the wilderness. The Puritans were the largest group to settle in Massachusetts. By 1640 there were over 20,000 colonists. The Puritans were determined to create a place where their strict religious beliefs could be practiced.

Religion was deeply important to the Puritans. They sought to receive saving grace from God, to become one of the "elect." Church attendance was required and absolute obedience to the stern morality of the church was expected of everyone. Ministers preached powerful sermons on the wonders of God and on the frightful prospects of damnation—burning for eternity in the horrors of hell. The Puritans would not tolerate those who did not follow their religious beliefs. The devil would do evil works, so each Puritan would have to take care.

One group of Puritans settled in Salem Village, now the city of Danvers, Massachusetts. Among this group began one of the grimmest episodes in the nation's history.

For young people life during the harsh New England winters was relentlessly boring. Thanksgiving was a happy celebration, but there were no other holidays to look forward to. Christmas was considered an immoral Catholic holiday, and its observance was forbidden for Puritans. For the young, especially the unmarried girls, there was little to do during the cold, dark winter. In the winter of 1691–1692, however, some girls found something to do—something secret, exciting, and terribly dangerous.

It began in the house of Reverend Samuel Parris, the stern local minister. His daughter Betty and her cousin Abigail, not yet in their teens, had heard his sermons about good and evil for as long as they could remember. From his slave woman, Tituba, they were to hear quite different messages.

Tituba was from the Barbados Islands where Rev. Parris had obtained her years earlier. She had been reared in a tradition of black magic, but of course could not talk about such things to a Puritan minister. In the flickering lights of the kitchen fire, however, the girls urged her to tell stories whenever Rev. Parris was out of the house.

Other girls and some young unmarried women became fascinated with Tituba's stories. Whenever possible they would sneak to Rev. Parris' house to hear her mysterious tales. Tituba seemed in touch with the mystical world of spirits. She told fortunes and, it was believed, could speak with the dead. The girls were awestruck but fearful. Fortune-telling was a sin and attempting to speak to the dead was punishable by death!

One day Betty fell mysteriously ill. She seemed in a trance. She stared blankly into space and babbled. Soon Abigail began strange behaviors: at times falling into a trance, at times crawling around barking like a dog, at times having convulsive fits. The local doctor could find no explanation, and soon it was believed the devil's hand was on them. A few years earlier a similar event occurred in Boston. A woman, believed to be a witch working with the devil, was hanged.

Ministers from surrounding towns were brought in to examine the girls. In the meantime, other girls had become afflicted. When prayers were offered, the girls' behavior became worse. There was no question. The devil was at work, and the girls would have to name who was tormenting them.

The girls were now the center of attention. They were constantly questioned and examined. Finally, in a delirious fit, Betty blurted out the name "Tituba." The others cried out their agreement and named two other women, Sarah Good and Sarah Osburne. All three of those named were taken to jail to await trial as witches.

The villagers were relieved. Both Sarah Good and Sarah Osburne were unpopular in the community. Good was a dirty beggar who smoked a pipe and Osburne, while not poor, had not been attending church for almost a year. Tituba believed in black magic. It seemed only right that these three would be witches.

Magistrates from Boston were sent to Salem to conduct pretrial examinations. These men were believed experts in determining if people were witches. There were a variety of tests, but the most important was based on the belief that the devil could not take the shape of an innocent person. If the girls saw shapes of people flying around causing harm, then those people must be guilty of working

with the devil. This evidence was called *spectral evidence*. It became
the basis for conviction. Anyone the girls claimed to have seen in their
visions could not be innocent.

On March 1, 1692, the first hearing was held in the church. The
villagers crowded in to watch. The girls sat in the front rows. When
the "witches" were brought in, the girls screamed and moaned, especially when Tituba was brought forward. The girls were probably
afraid that Tituba would tell the truth about their visits to her, but she
had been beaten by Rev. Parris and confessed a very different story.

For three days Tituba told of being taken over by the devil, who
made her shape fly around trying to cause harm. She had been to
witches' sabbaths and had seen red dogs and cats that could talk. A
"tall man" from Boston had appeared to her, and she had seen names
in his book. It must have been the devil's book. The magistrates asked
how many names she had seen. The crowd was stunned by her reply.
She had seen nine names! That meant there must be at least six more
witches in the area.

A cold wave of terror washed over the colony. The girls began
"crying out" on more and more people. Some of the most respected
members of the community were identified as witches. Even Rebecca
Nurse, a 71-year-old woman regarded as one of the most upstanding
church women, was accused.

Some began to doubt whether the girls should be believed. John
Proctor was one of them. He said if there were any devils in the area
they were the girls. Mary Warren, one of the girls and also Proctor's
maid, admitted to him that what the girls were doing was "for sport,"
but she would not say so publicly.

One day John Proctor would not allow Mary to go to the hearing, but he went with his wife, Elizabeth, who had been accused.
At the hearing the girls again wailed and moaned, and Abigail
identified Mr. Proctor as a wizard (a man working with the devil).
His life was now in danger.

Mr. and Mrs. Proctor were taken to jail and Mary was left to care
for the children. When the other girls heard that Mary had begun
telling the truth about them, they cried out that she, too, was a witch.
Mary was then hauled off to jail with the rest. In jail she was
questioned constantly. At first she denied that Mr. Proctor was a
wizard, but eventually she broke down and said that he was. She was
allowed to return to the accusing girls and never disagreed with them
again.

The girls became celebrities. People in other towns brought them in to identify any witches who might be haunting in their areas. If the girls claimed to see the shape of anyone flying about biting or choking people, then this person was deemed a witch or wizard. John Alden, son of the famous Priscilla and John, was named a wizard. George Burroughs, the former minister of Salem, was identified as the leader of the witches. No one was safe.

Life in the dank jails was horrid. The prisoners were chained and constantly questioned. In many cases they were tortured in an effort to get them to confess. Oddly, to confess meant that you would not be convicted of witchcraft. To deny truthfully that you were a witch would bring conviction—and the death sentence.

The first to die was Bridget Bishop. She was hanged on Gallows Hill in June 1692. Five more, including the frail, saintly Rebecca Nurse, were hanged on July 19. For those in jail there seemed little hope. Madness had taken hold in Massachusetts.

To confess could save your life, yet your property could be taken by the government. Old Giles Cory would not confess. He decided to say nothing at his trial. He correctly believed that if he stood mute his property would not be taken, and he could will it to his heirs. In attempting to get him to confess, the jailers set heavy rocks on his chest. Mr. Cory would not confess, and he was crushed to death. Some say his last words were: "more weight."

Many of the accused witches confessed to being witches. Some were so caught up in terror and fear that they may have actually believed they were witches. Some undoubtedly confessed to save their lives. Many would not confess, however, even though they knew they would hang on Gallows Hill.

Arthur Miller, in his powerful play *The Crucible*, captured the anguish of the accused. In the final scene, John Proctor is trying to decide whether he should confess. He is talking with his wife, Elizabeth, who although accused, will not be hanged because she is pregnant. A government official, Deputy Governor Danforth, is trying to make Mr. Proctor confess.

> PROCTOR (*with great force of will, but not quite looking at her*): I have been thinking I would confess to them, Elizabeth. (*She shows nothing.*) What say you? If I give them that?
>
> ELIZABETH: I cannot judge you, John. (*Pause*)

PROCTOR (*simply—a pure question*):   What would you have me do?

ELIZABETH: As you will I would have it. (*Slight pause*) I want you living John. That's sure.

. . .

PROCTOR: Then who will judge me? (*Suddenly clasping his hands*) God in heaven, what is John Proctor, what is John Proctor? (*He moves as an animal, and a fury is riding in him, a tantalized search.*) I think it is honest, I think so; I am no saint. (*As though she had denied this, he calls angrily at her.*) Let Rebecca go like a saint; for me it is fraud!!

. . .

DANFORTH: Mr. Proctor. When the Devil came to you did you see Rebecca Nurse in his company? (*Proctor is silent.*) Come, man, take courage —did you ever see her with the Devil?

PROCTOR (*almost inaudibly*):   No.

(*Danforth, now sensing trouble, glances at John and goes to the table and picks up a sheet—the list of condemned.*)

DANFORTH: Did you ever see her sister, Mary Easty, with the Devil?

PROCTOR: No, I did not.

DANFORTH (*his eyes narrow on Proctor*):   Did you ever see Martha Corey with the Devil?

PROCTOR: I did not.

. . .

DANFORTH: Mr. Proctor—

PROCTOR: You will not use me! I am no Sarah Good or Tituba. I am John Proctor! You will not use me! It is no part of salvation that you should use me!

DANFORTH: I do not wish to—

PROCTOR: I have three children—how may I teach them to walk like men in the world, and I sold my friends?

. . .

DANFORTH: Then explain to me, Mr. Proctor, why you will not
let—

PROCTOR (*with a cry of his whole soul*):   Because it is my name!
Because I cannot have another in my life! Because I lie and
sign myself to lies! Because I am not worth the dust on the
feet of them that hang! How may I live without my name?
I have given you my soul; leave me my name!

John Proctor would not confess. He was hanged with the others.
After a time the panic ended. Increasing numbers of people realized
that innocent people were being accused. The judges finally decided
that spectral evidence was no longer sufficient for conviction and the
girls' hysterical fantasies would not convict again.

The major sources for this story were:

Starkey, Marion L. *The Devil in Massachusetts*. Garden City, N.Y.: Anchor Books, 1969.
Miller, Arthur. *The Crucible*. New York: Viking Press, 1953, pp. 130, 132, 134, 137 138.

ACTIVITIES FOR "MADNESS IN MASSACHUSETTS"

Answer all questions on a separate sheet of paper.

Historical Understanding

Answer briefly:

1. How did the Puritan settlers differ from the Jamestown settlers?

2. Identify two major religious beliefs of the Puritans.

3. What were three difficulties faced by the early Puritan settlers?

Reviewing the Facts of the Case

Answer briefly:

1. Why wouldn't Tituba talk about black magic with Rev. Parris?

2. For what reason might the young girls and women have become
    fascinated with Tituba's stories? Why did they keep their meetings
    secret?

3. Why were the villagers relieved when the first few "witches" were named?

4. What was *spectral evidence*?

5. Why did the girls claim that Mary Warren was a witch?

6. Why didn't John Proctor confess?

Analyzing Ethical Issues

In this story there are a number of times that people made decisions involving the following values:

AUTHORITY: a value concerning what rules or people should be obeyed and the consequences for disobedience.

LIFE: a value concerning when, if ever, it is justifiable to threaten or take a life.

TRUTH: a value concerning the expression, distortion, or withholding of accurate information.

Indicate which of these values was involved in each of the following decisions, as illustrated in this example:

DECISION	VALUES INVOLVED
The girls decided to meet secretly with Tituba.	*Authority, Truth*

1. The judges decided to use spectral evidence at the trial.

2. John Proctor decided not to confess to witchcraft.

3. Mary Warren decided not to admit publicly what she had told John Proctor.

Expressing Your Reasoning

1. John Proctor faced a difficult dilemma. If he confessed he would be lying but it would save his life. Do you think he should have confessed? Why or why not?

2. Mary Warren told John Proctor the truth but refused to do so publicly. Do you think she should have told the truth publicly? Why or why not?

3. When Betty and Abigail began their sessions with Tituba they knew Rev. Parris would disapprove of what they were doing. Write a paragraph expressing your opinion of whether it was wrong of the girls to meet privately with Tituba. Include reasons for your opinion.

4. *Seeking Additional Information.* In making decisions about such questions as those above, we often feel we need more information before we are satisfied with our judgments. Choose one of the above questions about which you would want more information than is presented in the story. What additional information would you like? Why would that information help you make a more satisfactory decision?

Hatred on the Frontier

WHITES VS. INDIANS

Massacre of the American Indians at Lancaster by the Paxton Boys in 1763

As the population of the American colonies grew, more and more settlers moved westward. In the early 1700s, the western frontier of the colonies stretched roughly from western New York to Georgia. It was a hard life on the frontier. Settlers worked at felling trees and clearing the land for farming. It was also a dangerous life. The American Indians who resented the intrusion of the whites into their territories often fought with the settlers. The results of the bloodshed were terrible for both groups. In Georgia about one-half of the Cherokee population was killed off. During the first half of the century it was estimated that 2,000 settlers in western Pennsylvania were killed or captured.

The colonial westerners also came into conflict with the French. Much of the area between the Mississippi and the colonial frontier was controlled by the French. Throughout this area French fur traders did business with various tribes. Furs were popular in Europe, and the French, as well as some of the colonials, traded guns, tools, clothing, and rum for furs of animals trapped by the Indians.

The fur trade was often conducted honestly, but sometimes traders cheated the Indians. In one instance colonial traders gave a number of kegs of rum for furs. When the Indians returned to their village, they discovered the kegs were filled with water instead of rum. Naturally, Indians who were tricked or cheated became resentful toward whites.

Most of the conflict between Indians and colonial whites came over the control of land. Many Indians complained that whites were forcing them off the land that had traditionally belonged to their tribes for hunting and farming.

The British government tried to develop fair policies for dealing with Indian property rights, but these policies were difficult to enforce in the wilderness.

Tensions between Indians, British colonists, and French settlers led to battles and wars throughout the first half of the century. A major conflict erupted over control of the Ohio River Valley. It led to the French and Indian War of 1754–1763.

Throughout the war there were horrible instances of whites slaughtering and scalping Indians, and Indians scalping and slaughtering whites. One of the worst cases occurred in August 1757, at Fort William Henry in northern New York. The French general, Montcalm, with Indian allies from over 30 tribes, surrounded the fort. Lieutenant Colonel Monro, commander of the fort, was unable to get reinforcements and had to surrender. Montcalm had promised Monro that he and his men would be safe. It was not to be. At the time of the surrender, hundreds of Indians, inflamed by battle and rum drunk in victory celebrations, massacred most of the unarmed prisoners.

Hatred between Indians and whites increased in 1763 as a result of Pontiac's Uprising. Pontiac, the brilliant Ottawa chieftain, believed it was time to push back the colonial whites. Many other tribes agreed. All along the frontier occurred some of the most fierce Indian-white battles of the century.

The settlers in western Pennsylvania suffered greatly during these times. Their growing hatred of Indians was matched by their disgust with the government back east in Philadelphia. The settlers were convinced their government was failing them.

For one thing, the settlers did not believe they were fairly represented in the elected assembly. By 1760 there were five western counties in the Pennsylvania colony. Because of an old system of representation, the eastern counties had almost three times as many representatives in the assembly as did the western counties. This system was in effect even though the population of eligible voters in the east and west was about equal.

There was also religious hostility. Most of the settlers were Scotch-Irish Presbyterians. Throughout Pennsylvania there were many different religious groups, but the government was controlled by the Quakers, the religion of the colony's founder, William Penn.

The Quakers in the east did not fully understand the problems of the frontier settlers. Also, their religious beliefs opposed violence. The Quakers, through their Association, gave gifts and friendship to Indian tribes that they believed were friendly and not at war. Many of the settlers were angered at this practice. They claimed it was not easy to tell friendly from enemy tribes.

The settlers also believed the government did not do enough to protect them during the wars. At one point, settlers brought wagonloads of their dead neighbors to Philadelphia. The wagons were driven through the streets to dramatize the settlers' need for protection. In spite of these demonstrations and requests from British military leaders, the assembly never voted enough money for troops to satisfy the settlers and the British.

The horrors of war and the political disputes with Philadelphia formed the background for a series of events that, some believe, almost led to civil war in Pennsylvania.

The winter of 1763 was harsh on the frontier. Battles with Indians were severe. Men, women, and children were killed. Hatred and fear consumed both Indians and whites. A group of settlers at the town of Paxton on the Susquehanna River took brutal action.

At Conestoga, about 50 miles from Paxton, lived a group of Indians. The Paxton men were convinced that the Conestoga Indians, who appeared to be living in peace with the whites, had provided aid to enemy tribes. They also believed that one of the Indians had murdered a white woman. On December 14, 1763, Matthew Smith and a group of other settlers attacked the Conestoga Indians and killed three men, two women, and one child.

News of the massacre shocked eastern officials. The Conestoga Indians had been living in peace and had made their living by selling baskets and brooms. Governor John Penn ordered the capture of the murderers, and the assembly voted to provide protection for any Indians who requested it.

The government's response further inflamed the Paxton men. When they heard that fourteen of the surviving Indians were being housed, for their protection, at a jail in Lancaster, they galloped to that town. The Paxtons claimed that one of the Indians was a murderer but, in their rage, they attacked the jail and killed all the Indians.

Eastern officials were horrified. Governor Penn offered a reward of 200 pounds for the capture of any of the leaders of the Paxton Boys. In addition, about one hundred and twenty-five Indians were brought into Philadelphia to be protected at a military barracks.

Not all the citizens of Philadelphia supported this move. Many were sympathetic to the Paxtons. Crowds shouted insults at the Indians when they were brought into the city. One observer claimed that a clear majority of the Philadelphians opposed protecting the Indians in the city.

The Paxton Boys were in a frenzy. In taverns and stores they could talk of little other than the Indian massacres and unacceptable government policies. How could the government that had not given them enough protection now decide to protect Indians? A plan was made to attack the Indians in the city. If any Philadelphians stood in the way they too might be killed.

News of the coming attack caused panic in Philadelphia. There were rumors that 5,000 rough frontiersmen were going to invade the city. About a thousand citizens joined a volunteer militia. Barricades were built for the streets. A system of warning bells was put into effect. When the bells rang, the volunteers would take their weapons to key points in the city. One night there was a false alarm, and armed citizens waited through the cold winter night for an attack that never came.

Not long afterward in February 1764, the Paxton Boys marched to Philadelphia. They stopped outside the city at Germantown. About two hundred and fifty tough frontiersmen carrying rifles and tomahawks were in the group. The rumor that thousands would arrive proved incorrect.

Philadelphia officials met to decide what to do. In an effort to head off conflict, Benjamin Franklin and some other leading Philadelphians were sent to speak to the Paxton leaders. After hearing the complaints of the Paxtons, Franklin and the others promised that the government would seriously and quickly consider their requests. As a result of the promise, most of the Paxton Boys returned to their homes. Matthew Smith and a few stayed behind to write up their requests for government action. Armed conflict had been prevented.

The Paxton Boys asked the government to do a number of things. Among their requests were: (1) more military protection for the frontier, (2) equal representation for the western counties in the assembly, and (3) a system of payments for Indian scalps. Payment for scalps had been provided by the government in earlier Indian wars. The payments were designed to encourage frontiersmen to do battle with the Indians thus helping the military. The policy had been discontinued, but the Paxton Boys wanted it to begin again.

In spite of the promises, the government had no intention of seriously considering the Paxton requests. Most of the officials were disgusted with the actions of the frontiersmen. Benjamin Franklin later called the Paxtons cowards and madmen. Some officials thought the requests were an attempt to divert attention from the massacres. They thought the requests were intended to cover up savage behavior. Other officials did not want to change the system of representation because they feared the frontier would get too much power in government. The government did not act directly on any of the Paxton Boys' requests.

Later in the summer of 1764, however, battles associated with Pontiac's Uprising led the governor to offer rewards for the scalps of any Indians over the age of ten. In March of 1776, 12 years after the Paxton March, the western counties received equal representation in the assembly.

The Indians in Philadelphia were gradually returned to the frontier. None of the Paxton Boys was ever brought to trial for the massacres.

The major sources for this story were:

Hindle, Brooke. "The March of the Paxton Boys." *The William and Mary Quarterly*, October 1946, pp. 461 486.

Jacobs, Wilber R. *The Paxton Riots and the Frontier Theory.* The Berkeley Series in American History. Chicago: Rand McNally, 1967.

ACTIVITIES FOR "HATRED ON THE FRONTIER"

Answer all questions on a separate sheet of paper.

Historical Understanding

Answer briefly:

1. Identify two causes of conflict between the American colonists and various American Indian tribes.

2. What was one underlying factor that led to tension between eastern and western colonists in Pennsylvania?

3. What triggered the French and Indian War?

Reviewing the Facts of the Case

Answer briefly:

1. Why did the Paxton Boys attack the Indians at Conestoga and Lancaster?

2. How did the Philadelphia government respond to the attacks?

3. What promise did Franklin and the others make to the Paxtons?

4. What were the requests of the Paxtons?

Analyzing Ethical Issues

There are a number of incidents in this story involving the following values:

EQUALITY: a value concerning whether people should be treated in the same way.

LIFE: a value concerning when, if ever, it is justifiable to threaten or take a life.

PROPERTY: a value concerning what people should be allowed to own and how they should be allowed to use it.

TRUTH: a value concerning the expression, distortion, or with-holding of accurate information.

For each of the values above—equality, life, property, and truth—write a sentence describing an incident from the story involving that value, as illustrated in this example:

Equality: *The Paxtons believed that the colonial government provided better protection for the Indians than it did for western settlers.*

Expressing Your Reasoning

1. Benjamin Franklin and other leaders promised they would quickly and seriously consider the Paxtons' requests. Was it right to make the promise even though they did not intend to keep it? Why or why not?

2. The Pennsylvania government authorized the protection of some of the Indians. Was it right to protect the Indians in the city? Why or why not?

3. The Paxtons wanted a reward for Indian scalps. Later in the year Governor Penn offered a reward for the scalps of enemy Indians. In a paragraph express your judgment of the Governor's action. Indicate whether or not you agree with him and support your position with reasons.

4. *Seeking Additional Information.* In making decisions about such questions as those above, we often feel we need more information before we are satisfied with our judgments. Choose one of the above questions about which you would want more information than is presented in the story. What additional information would you like? Why would that information help you make a more satisfactory decision?

A Sticky Business

COLONIAL SMUGGLING

Destruction of the Schooner Gaspee

If you walked along the docks of colonial cities like Boston, New York, or Charleston in the mid-1700s you would see the tall masts of many wooden trading ships. Sailors and longshoremen would be busy at work in the brisk salt air. In some cases, especially in Boston, you might see a British warship at anchor. Here and there small groups of people might be intently whispering. You might feel an ugly tension. You might even see an angry mob yelling at officials and hurling stones at them.

This hostility was mainly a result of England's attempt to enforce laws against smuggling. It was illegal to bring certain goods into the colonies without paying a fee called a *duty*. Many colonial merchants tried to avoid paying the duty because they could make more money if they didn't pay it. Sneaking dutied goods into the colonies was smuggling, and the British attempt to control it was a factor that led to the American Revolution.

England and other colonial powers like Spain, Portugal, France, and Holland practiced an economic policy called *mercantilism*. Simply put, this policy meant that a colony could trade only with its corresponding colonial power and its orbit of other colonies. Colonies were to supply raw materials to the colonial power and buy from it manufactured goods and other products. They were supposed to exist for the benefit of the colonial power. In return, the colonial power would provide protection for the colonies. Mercantilism was the accepted policy of the times.

Colonial merchants were interested in making money. It was highly profitable to trade with the islands in the West Indies. Ships carried lumber, flour, and other goods to the British colonies there in return for sugar, molasses, and other products. Back in New England the molasses was distilled into rum. The rum was then sold or taken to Africa where it was traded for slaves. Slaves were brought to the West Indies or the southern colonies where they were sold or traded. This trade route, from New England to West Africa to the West Indies and back to New England, is an example of what is known as *triangular trade*.

According to mercantile laws, the colonial traders were only to deal with the British islands, such as Jamaica. The traders, however, found it more profitable to get molasses from other islands such as those owned by the French. The products of these foreign islands were often 25 to 40 percent less expensive than those of the British islands. Also, the foreign islands were eager to get all the American products they could get.

To prevent American trade with the foreign islands, Parliament passed the Molasses Act of 1733. According to this law, any foreign molasses brought into the colonies would be charged a sixpence per gallon duty. It was believed that this duty would make trade in foreign molasses too expensive for the Americans and force them to deal only with the British islands. In fact, the law was not well enforced and many merchants smuggled in the foreign molasses.

When a ship entered a colonial harbor, the captain was supposed to tell customs officials what products were on board. If dutied goods were on the ship, the duty would have to be paid before the cargo could be delivered. Because the law was poorly enforced, shipowners found many ways to avoid paying. Cargo reports would be falsified to indicate few or no dutied goods on board. Packages would be mis-labeled. Customs officials were often bribed or threatened with violence to keep them from inspecting cargoes. Also, because of the extensive American coastline, it was often possible for captains to unload their ships away from the main harbors.

Because it was easy to avoid paying the duties, smuggling was widespread. To many, smuggling was the normal way of doing business. The French and Indian War changed all that.

From 1754–1763, thousands of British soldiers fought in America in an attempt to safeguard the westward expansion of the colonies and to end the colonists' conflict with the French and their American Indian allies. The war was extremely costly for the British in both lives and money.

During the war, American smugglers continued to trade with the French islands. In fact, some new routes were opened. The British were outraged because such trade helped the enemy get food and other supplies. Some claimed the trade helped prolong the war. It certainly increased its costs. For example, the large amounts of flour shipped to the French made the cost of colonial bread very high. At one point the British army found it cheaper to bring supplies all the way from England than to buy them in the colonies.

Prime Minister William Pitt, usually sympathetic to the concerns of the colonists, believed the colonies should help pay for the costs of the war and their own protection. When George Grenville became prime minister in 1763, a series of policies were adopted intended to get the colonies to pay. The Sugar Act of 1764 was, in part, an attempt to raise money and to cut down on colonial smuggling by reforming the old Molasses Act.

According to the Sugar Act, a threepence per gallon duty on foreign molasses would be strictly enforced. More customs officials would be sent to the colonies and the British navy would be authorized to help in enforcement. There would also be rewards for colonists who informed officials about smugglers. The money raised by this law was to help pay for the cost of military protection in the colonies.

Strict enforcement of the law decreased the smuggling of molasses. Smuggling in other goods, such as tea, continued. Tension between the colonists and the officials increased as additional laws were passed and enforcement stiffened. A Rhode Island customs official, Jesse Saville, was beaten severely and then tarred and feathered. One night a Massachusetts official was awakened at gunpoint and forced to reveal the name of an informer.

Resentment against the new British laws made smuggling seem like a noble act to some. When the colonial trading ship *Liberty* was seized by Boston custom officials in June of 1768, a dockside mob threw stones at the British sailors who were towing it away. The mob then rioted, causing substantial damage to the homes of the customs officials. In 1772, the British ship *Gaspee*, which had been patrolling for smugglers, ran aground near Providence, Rhode Island. A group of colonists, led by the wealthy merchant John Brown, seized the crew and burned the ship. It was estimated that at least a thousand local residents knew the names of those who attacked the ship but, when British investigators arrived, not a single witness would identify the attackers.

The early British laws had been designed to regulate trade according to the principles of mercantilism. At first there had been no significant or widespread objection from the colonies. After the French and Indian War, however, the flurry of new laws was resented. To many, the new duties seemed like taxes levied on the colonies without their consent. Colonial boycotts, petitions, and riots brought no major change in British policy. A revolutionary struggle was to come.

The major sources for this story were:

McClellan, William S. *Smuggling in the American Colonies*. New York: Moffat, Yard, 1912.
Schlesinger, Arthur M. *Colonial Merchants and the American Revolution*. New York: Frederick Ungar, 1957.

ACTIVITIES FOR "A STICKY BUSINESS"

Answer all questions on a separate sheet of paper.

Historical Understanding

Answer briefly:

1. Define the following: *duty* and *mercantilism.*

2. Why was smuggling profitable?

3. Why was the British Parliament concerned about smuggling?

4. Why did the British try to enforce the Sugar Act after the French and Indian War?

5. What was *triangular trade?*

Reviewing the Facts of the Case

Answer briefly:

1. Why did some merchants trade with the French colonies in the West Indies even though it was illegal?

2. Why was the Molasses Act passed?

3. What were two ways shipowners could avoid paying duties?

4. What was the purpose of the Sugar Act?

5. What happened after the ship *Liberty* was seized by customs officials?

6. What happened when the British ship *Gaspee* ran aground?

Analyzing Ethical Issues

There is agreement on the answer to some questions. For other questions there is disagreement about the answer. We call these questions issues. Issues can be categorized as factual or ethical. A factual issue asks whether something is true or false, accurate or inaccurate. An ethical issue asks whether something is right or wrong, fair or unfair. Factual issues ask what *is*; ethical issues ask what *ought to be*.

For each of the following questions decide whether the issue is factual or ethical, as illustrated in this example:

> Could the British have paid for the French and Indian War without passing the Sugar Act? *Factual.*
>
> Should Rhode Island residents have told British authorities who was responsible for burning the *Gaspee*? *Ethical.*

1. Could colonial merchants always make more money if they engaged in smuggling?

2. Was mercantilism accepted by most people during the 1700s?

3. Should the British have tried to enforce the Molasses Act?

4. Were the British right in expecting the colonists to pay for the cost of war?

5. Did colonial smuggling prolong the French and Indian War?

6. Was smuggling a leading cause of the American Revolution?

Expressing Your Reasoning

1. Were colonial traders right to engage in smuggling? Why or why not? There are many arguments that can be made for and against colonial smuggling. For each of the following indicate if you think it is a strong or weak argument. Explain your thinking.
   a. Before 1763 the British did not enforce the laws against smuggling very strongly. Therefore, smuggling at that time was normal and not wrong to do.
   b. The colonists were really British citizens and were obligated to obey the laws of Parliament. Therefore, smuggling was wrong because it was illegal.
   c. Smuggling allowed the merchants to make more profits in their businesses and they had a right to make as much money as possible.
   d. Smuggling was wrong during the French and Indian War because it helped the French get supplies.

    e. Trading with foreign islands allowed less expensive goods to come into the colonies so all the people could live more cheaply.

    f. The colonists should not have smuggled because they had an obligation to help pay the costs of the British army.

    g. After the war the British policies were too severe. Smuggling was right because it was a protest against unfair policy.

    h. Smuggling was wrong because it led to other wrong practices like bribery, lying, and violence.

    i. Smuggling was wrong because it forced Parliament to pass severe laws like the Sugar Act.

2. Rhode Island residents refused to tell British investigators who was responsible for the burning of the *Gaspee*. Were they wrong in not telling? Why or why not? Write a paragraph explaining your point of view.

3. *Seeking Additional Information.* In making decisions about such questions as those above, we often feel we need more information before we are satisfied with our judgments. Choose one of the above questions about which you would like more information than is presented in the story. What additional information would you like? Why would that information help you make a more satisfactory decision?

Defending the Redcoats

JOHN ADAMS

(Courtesy, The Henry Francis du Pont Winterthur Museum)

The Bloody Massacre

(Courtesy, the Massachusetts Historical Society)

John Adams Portrait

The decade of the 1760s was a period of growing tension between England and its American colonies. By defeating France in the French and Indian War (1754–1763), England secured its control of the colonies. The war, however, left Britain with a staggering debt. In desperate need of funds England thought the Americans should contribute to the costs of the empire. Attempts to tax the colonists triggered events that led to revolution.

England tried to raise revenue in the colonies by collecting *customs duties*, which were taxes placed on goods imported from abroad. Another name for them is a *tariff*. To avoid paying the tariff many Americans became smugglers. They slipped foreign goods into the colonies without paying the customs duties. Customs officials of the Crown obtained written court orders, called Writs of Assistance, that enabled them to conduct general searches for smuggled goods. A group of Massachusetts merchants challenged the writs in court but lost their case. Smuggling continued.

In 1764 Parliament passed the Sugar Act. Its purpose was to collect tax on molasses imported by the colonies from the West Indies. Smugglers had evaded previous duties on molasses. To ensure that the new tax would be collected, the act placed special courts in the major American seaports. These courts had no juries. Naval judges examined the evidence, weighed guilt, and passed sentence. Strict enforcement of the new act raised the price of sugar, which embittered the colonists.

It was not only higher prices that angered the colonists. They were also concerned with their lack of political power. They objected to being regulated or taxed by a foreign legislature in which they had no elected representatives. This arrangement gave rise to the now famous protest slogan, "No taxation without representation."

Though American opposition was already aroused by the Sugar Act, the search for revenue by the Crown led Parliament to pass the Stamp Act in 1765. This act placed a tax on various goods and services produced within the colonies. The tax was paid by purchasing a stamp that was then placed on the article. Stamps were required for such items as newspapers, leases, playing cards, legal documents, and advertisements.

The colonial reaction to the Stamp Act was swift and violent. On August 14, 1765, Andrew Oliver, the Crown-appointed stamp collector, had his effigy hung on a huge tree in central Boston that became known as the Liberty Tree. That evening a mob dragged the effigy to Oliver's elegant town house where they broke down the door and forced their way in. His furniture was destroyed and his family terrorized.

Twelve days later a raucous crowd made its way to the mansion of the colonial governor, Thomas Hutchinson. Hutchinson was dining with his wife and children. The crowd split the door with axes, plundering and gutting the house. They destroyed what they could not take away—china, rugs, clocks, furniture, and family portraits. Nothing remained but the roof, bare walls, and the floor.

Rioters in many cities prevented collection of the stamp tax. Prominent Bostonians denounced Parliament's authority to tax the colonies without consent. Some of these protesters, led by Sam Adams, organized a group called the Sons of Liberty. Their aim was to turn street violence into political action.

Parliament soon repealed the Stamp Act. In doing so, however, it declared full power to pass laws or levy taxes for America "in all cases whatsoever." Sentiment for colonial self-government continued to grow, especially in Boston.

Soon after repealing the Stamp Act, Parliament levied the Townshend Taxes. These taxes levied a customs duty on various colonial imports such as paint, tea, paper, lead, and glass. The revenue from these taxes was to be used to pay the salaries of colonial governors. Until this time colonists had paid these salaries. A salary paid by the Crown would eliminate the only power the colonists had over the governor. The Sons of Liberty and their supporters insisted that the power to collect taxes belonged to the colonial assemblies, not to the Crown.

Some merchants refused to import British goods until the Townshend Taxes were repealed. They considered the import taxes intolerable. Resentment was extremely high in Boston where violence broke out again. The British responded firmly by sending two regiments of royal troops to the city. This began a military occupation of Boston. Two opposing forces were moving toward collision.

The new prime minister in England, Lord North, had little sympathy for American problems. He once referred to protesting colonists as "the drunken ragamuffins of a vociferous mob." He is also quoted as saying, "I can never acquiesce in the absurd opinion that all men are equal."

British soldiers, in their bright red coats, were the visible objects of Boston's bitterness. The redcoats marched up King Street in Boston with drums beating, fifes playing, and colors flying.

Antagonism between citizen and soldier flared repeatedly. One night in February 1770, Christopher Snider joined some other boys shouting outside the home of a customs official. In response to the boys' taunts the customs collector stomped out of his door. Armed, he fired his musket into the crowd of boys. Christopher Snider, just 12 years old, fell dead. One of those who witnessed the boy's funeral the next day was John Adams.

During these times of conflict between the Crown and its colonies, John Adams, a talented lawyer in his thirties, was building a career in Boston. He had recently moved his family from their small farm in Braintree to a house in Boston, closer to his law practice. As he rode the circuit court trying cases or walked the streets of the city, he was recognized as a "patriot" lawyer. He was often invited to dine and discuss events sweeping the American colonies. Though not as radical as the Sons of Liberty, John Adams sympathized with their cause.

The early months of 1770 were a melancholy period for John Adams, then 34 years old. His wife, Abigail, usually strong and competent about the house, was not herself. She did not complain but was that winter unusually quiet, almost listless. When John came home those cold afternoons, he often found her sitting in the dark gazing out the window. When he tried to engage her in conversation, Abigail turned away her head to hide the tears. John felt uneasy, leaving her alone in the house with her two maids. The new houseboy was unreliable, rarely at hand when needed. These were dark days for Abigail, and John planned to begin spending more time with her than he normally did.

The Adams's daughter, Susanna, scarcely a year old, had died just after Christmas. Abigail was pregnant with a baby expected in May. The couple's other two children, ages five and three, needed their father's attention more than usual because their mother was feeling so low.

So it was for John Adams during the winter of 1770 as the clouds of discontent gathered over Boston. Ever since troops had assembled in the city there was a growing dread of an explosion. The image of the troops in the Bay Colony had changed quickly from "His Majesty's Dignified Regulars" into one of bullies and outlaws hired abroad to cut off any chance of resistance. Soldiers were subjected to daily insults and abuse on the streets: "Lobsters for sale . . . lo-obsters, who'll buy," crowds jeered at the redcoats. The soldiers cursed and spat. "Yankees!" they called back.

On the morning of March 4, 1770, a poster appeared, tacked up near the waterfront:

> This is to inform the rebellious people in Boston that the soldyers in the 14th and 29th Regiments are determined to join together and defend themselves against all who shall oppose them.
>
> Signed,
> the soldyers of the 14th and 29th
> Regiments

No one ever found out who posted the sign. Some believe it was not the soldiers but the Sons of Liberty.

The climactic conflict finally came in Boston the night of March 5, 1770. It was a chilly moonlit evening with a foot of packed snow on the ground. Down King Street, Private Hugh White of the Twenty-ninth British Regiment walked his solitary post. As Private White stood near his sentry box a group of rowdies jeered at him until he lost his temper and knocked one of them down with his musket butt. The commotion drew a crowd. White became a target for snowballs, chunks of ice, and lumps of coal. Frightened, he hurried to the Customs House. He found the door locked as the surging crowd shouted, "Kill him, kill him!"

The crowd threatened to overcome the lone redcoat. Captain Thomas Preston, officer in charge, heard the uproar and led a relief party of seven soldiers to the rescue. At bayonet point Preston's group forced its way through the throng to reach White. Forming a line alongside White, the soldiers were showered with flying objects, catcalls, and taunts.

Some of the soldiers' faces were bloodied. One private, clubbed into the gutter, scrambled to his feet, shouted out, "Damn you, fire!" and pulled the trigger of his musket. The shot hit no one, but the other soldiers began firing. When the smoke cleared, five men lay sprawled in the snow, three dead and two others mortally wounded. The stillness was then broken by the thud and rattle of rammers as the soldiers loaded their guns once again. Captain Preston then ordered his men to withdraw across the street. The wounded and dead were carried away.

Suddenly, all over the city, bells began to ring the alarm. An angry crowd of men appeared on the streets carrying any weapons they could find. Cries of "To arms!" echoed through the streets. Governor Thomas Hutchinson came immediately to King Street.

The governor struggled through the throng until he reached the State House. He appeared on the balcony, facing in the moonlight a seething, roaring, angry mass that filled the square below. Governor Hutchinson stood a moment and waited. "Go home," he said at last. "Let the law settle this thing! Let the law have its course. I myself will live and die by the law. Let you also keep to this principle. Blood has been shed; awful work was done this night. Tomorrow there will be an inquiry." The crowd slowly dispersed. By three o'clock in the morning it was over.

Before sunrise a court of inquiry issued warrants for the arrest of Captain Preston and the eight soldiers. They were jailed to await their trial for murder. Sam Adams, leader of the Sons of Liberty, had already dubbed the incident the Horrid Massacre. Events of the night have survived in history as the Boston Massacre.

John Adams had heard sounds of violence the night before in the streets. He hurried home concerned about the safety of his family. The next morning he was met at his law office by a stranger named James Forest, a loyalist and friend of the accused British officer, Captain Preston.

Mr. Forest had just been with Captain Preston in jail. "Why are you here?" asked John Adams. Breathing hard, Mr. Forest begged Mr. Adams to undertake Captain Preston's defense. "His life is in danger," claimed Mr. Forest. "He has no one to defend him. Mr. Adams, would you consider—will you take his case?" Mr. Forest almost sobbed. The words came out in a rush. He had come to John Adams for two reasons: he could find no other lawyer to take the case, and Mr. Adams had a reputation for being a fair and decent man.

The implications of the decision facing John Adams staggered him. All other lawyers in the city had refused to defend Captain Preston or the other eight soldiers. They feared for their own lives if it became public that they were defending the redcoats. John Adams pondered the importance of having due process of law and impartial justice in the colonies. He expected that this trial would prove as important a case as had been tried in any court of any country in the world.

Walking home to dinner that night John Adams was thinking about his dilemma. A group of Sons of Liberty stopped him on the street and warned him against defending "those murderers." *Tories* (those loyal to the Crown) in Boston urged him to take the case. "Nine Tories out of ten," John told Abigail gloomily, "are convinced I have come over to their side." He was greatly disturbed at the thought that his own friends, the liberty group, would scorn him and that the loyalists would regard him a hero if he decided to take the case.

John learned that Governor Hutchinson was determined, should a jury convict, to urge a King's pardon for all eight men. On the other hand, John Adams' skill might actually persuade the jury to bring a verdict of not guilty. The governor preferred a verdict of not guilty to a royal pardon. If John Adams took the case, he wondered whether he would be viewed as a loyalist sympathizer doing the bidding of King George III.

Arriving at home one evening, he found a window broken. Abigail showed him two rocks she had picked up in the room. It was clear to John that if he accepted the case, his house and family would be placed in jeopardy.

The case would be difficult to win. It soon became known that of the 96 witnesses prepared to testify, 94 made it appear that the fault lay entirely with the soldiers.

It would take a defense lawyer a great deal of time to prepare to challenge their testimony. If John took the case, the months before the trial would be wholly taken up in preparation. The trial itself would last a long time. John feared bankruptcy if all his time were taken up with this trial. Little time would be left for other legal work and the handsome fees collected for it. Clearly, accepting the case would require financial sacrifice for John Adams.

John Adams wanted to make an honest fortune for himself and his family, to improve his small farm, and to educate his children. Were he to take on the harassing job of defending the redcoats he would be taking a different course. Besides, his family had special need of him at home these days.

Another thought occurred to John. In the back of his mind he had considered a career in politics. What chance would he have of being elected to the legislature if he accepted the unpopular job of defending the British soldiers?

England certainly, and perhaps all Europe, would be watching the trial. John said to his friend Josiah Quincy, "It will serve our enemies well if we publish proof that the people's cause in America is led by a mere mob, a riotous and irresponsible waterfront rabble."

If John Adams took the case, most townspeople would think he was trying to screen murderers from justice. Yet, were the British not entitled to be defended against the charge of murder? John Adams struggled to reach a decision.

The major sources for this story were:

Adams, John Quincy, and Adams, Charles Francis. *The Life of John Adams*. Philadelphia: J. B. Lippincott, 1871.
Bowen, Catherine. *John Adams and the American Revolution*. Boston: Little, Brown, 1950.
Russell, Francis. *Adams, An American Dynasty*. New York: American Heritage, 1976.
Shepard, Jack. *The Adams Chronicles*. Boston: Little, Brown, 1975.

ACTIVITIES FOR "DEFENDING THE REDCOATS"

Answer all questions on a separate sheet of paper.

Historical Understanding

Answer briefly:

1. What did the Writs of Assistance, the Sugar Act, the Stamp Act, and the Townshend Taxes all have in common?

2. Explain what the Sons of Liberty meant by the protest slogan "No taxation without representation."

3. Why were British troops stationed in Boston?

4. What was the Boston Massacre?

Reviewing the Facts of the Case

Answer briefly:

1. Identify two events that led to violence in Boston on King Street the night of March 5, 1770.

2. Why was John Adams especially concerned about his family at the time of the Boston Massacre?

3. Why did James Forest seek out John Adams to serve as the defense lawyer for the British soldiers accused of murder?

4. Why did Adams think this trial would draw attention in other parts of the world?

Analyzing Ethical Issues

There is agreement on the answer to some questions. For other questions there is disagreement about the answer. We call these questions issues. Issues can be categorized as factual or ethical. A factual issue asks whether something is true or false, accurate or inaccurate. An ethical issue asks whether something is right or wrong, fair or unfair. Factual issues ask what *is*; ethical issues ask what *ought to be*.

For each of the following questions decide whether the issue is factual or ethical, as illustrated in this example:

> During the 1760s did most of the citizens of Boston object to the Stamp Act? *Factual.*
>
> Was it right for colonial merchants to smuggle goods into the colonies without paying customs duties? *Ethical.*

1. If the British soldiers were convicted of murder would they be pardoned by the Crown?

2. Should the colonies have been granted representatives in the British Parliament?

3. Did Captain Preston order his troops to fire on the colonists?

4. Were the redcoats acting out of self-defense when they fired into the crowd?

5. Was it right for Boston merchants to boycott British imports after the Townshend Taxes were levied?

6. Was it fair for customs officials to search homes of suspected smugglers?

7. Did the Sons of Liberty think John Adams ought to defend the British soldiers?

8. Did the colonists have a moral obligation to pay part of the costs of the empire?

Expressing Your Reasoning

1. Should John Adams have accepted the job of defending the British soldiers? State the best reason you have in support of your position.

2. John Adams did accept the case. All eight British soldiers were found not guilty of murder. Two of them, however, were convicted of manslaughter. Suppose John Adams had decided not to take the case. Which of the following would have been his best reason for not taking the case? Explain your thinking.
   a. Taking the case would have required John to neglect his family during a period when they needed his time and attention.

b. By accepting the case John would have risked being attacked by angry townsmen or of having his house vandalized.

c. John would have lost a lot of income by spending so much time preparing and trying the case.

d. John might have hurt his political future by becoming known as the lawyer who tried to get the Crown's soldiers off the hook.

e. The liberty group in Boston was emerging as the chosen leaders of the people. As a faithful member of that group, John ought not to have done anything to undermine their influence.

f. The troops were in Boston by order of the King and Parliament. Local citizens considered the soldiers unlawful foreign occupiers. The colonists did not consent to have the troops stationed in the city. Therefore, the soldiers were not entitled to the protection of the colonial courts, or a lawyer to defend them.

3. Before the trial began John Adams came to believe that the soldiers were innocent of the charge of murder. Suppose John had believed the soldiers were guilty as charged? Should he still have accepted the case? Why or why not? Write a paragraph expressing your opinion.

4. *Seeking Additional Information.* In making decisions about such questions as those above, we often feel we need more information before we are satisfied with our judgments. Choose one of the above questions about which you would want more information than is presented in the story. What additional information would you like? Why would that information help you make a more satisfactory decision?

From Triumph to Treason

BENEDICT ARNOLD

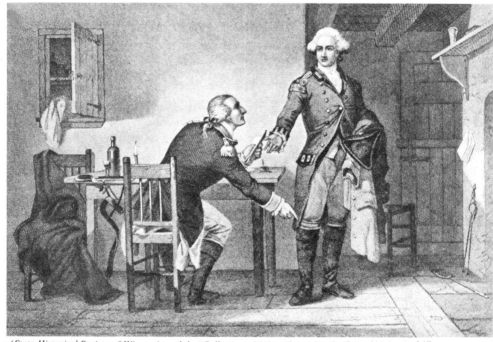

(State Historical Society of Wisconsin and the "Collection of Prints Illustrating the Fate of Major André")

Treason of Arnold

On any list of great villains in American history the name Benedict Arnold is likely to appear. Even today to call someone "a Benedict Arnold" is equivalent to calling that person a traitor. Strangely, however, on any list of great military heroes of the American Revolution, the name Benedict Arnold is also likely to appear. According to one historian: "Arnold was easily the outstanding battlefield officer of the Revolution." How odd it seems that a man can be both a hero and a villain. What did he do to bring about such contradictory judgments?

Stormy issues swept through America at the time of the Revolution. Many people were not certain that the Revolution should be fought. State governments wanted to protect their own authority. They were suspicious of one another as well as the Continental Congress. The congress was trying to establish greater authority over the separate states. There were also the practical problems of finding effective military leaders and raising enough money to support the American army. Benedict Arnold's life was deeply affected by these difficulties.

At the beginning of the Revolution, Arnold was an energetic, patriotic businessman in New Haven, Connecticut. Although the death of his parents had left him with little money, he had become fairly wealthy in the business of trading with Canada and the West Indies. In addition, he was happily married to Peggy Mansfield, a member of one of Connecticut's most prominent families.

British trade restrictions hurt many businessmen like Arnold. He came to believe that military action against the British was both necessary and right. After the news that war with England had begun, Arnold was elected to lead a group of soldiers to Boston. Once there he convinced the Massachusetts officials that they needed cannons to help drive the British out of the city. Where to get the cannons? The poorly defended British Fort Ticonderoga in New York had many, and could easily be attacked. At first the Massachusetts group was unwilling to send troops because they thought the New York government would protest an "invasion" from Massachusetts. Finally they supported Arnold's idea and sent him to New York. Arnold was pleased. Not only had they accepted his plan; they had also promoted him to colonel.

Things did not go as smoothly as Colonel Arnold hoped. A Connecticut group had also decided the cannons of Ticonderoga should be captured and sent to Boston. They supplied money to the rough-and-ready Ethan Allen and his Green Mountain Boys for an attack on the fort. Allen and Arnold met and had a raging argument over who should command the attack. Finally they compromised and agreed to share leadership.

The fort was taken without bloodshed. In spite of Arnold's significant role in the victory, friends of Allen sent an account of the battle to Massachusetts. Their story made it appear that Ethan Allen deserved all the credit for the victory. This would not be the last time that Arnold's pride and reputation would be insulted by unfair accusations. The worst was yet to come.

Arnold's pride was hurt and so was his bank account. Massachusetts had not provided enough money for the mission and Arnold helped pay for his troops with his own money. In spite of this the Massachusetts committee was unwilling to pay him back. If this weren't enough, Arnold learned that his beloved wife had died leaving his three young sons without a mother.

One man did give Arnold the credit he deserved—General George Washington. Washington recognized Arnold's ability and sent him on a mission to capture Quebec. To avoid squabbles between the politicians in different states, Washington placed Arnold directly under his command.

In September 1775, Arnold, with an army of about one thousand, began the long march to Quebec. The plan was to leave from Massachusetts and march hundreds of miles through unmapped Maine wilderness. Arnold's leadership was extraordinary. Harsh weather, floods, and disease afflicted his troops. One of his officers and an entire division deserted and returned to Boston.

In spite of these hardships Arnold and his remaining troops reached the St. Lawrence River. His heroic efforts were praised by Washington. Arnold's men also admired his courageous leadership.

Although the grueling march through Maine was a success, the attempt to capture Quebec was not. From an American deserter the troops at Quebec had learned of the coming attack. They were prepared. Also, Arnold was supposed to receive supplies and more troops from an American army at Montreal. For various reasons he received neither. Arnold's attempt to take Quebec failed. During the fierce fighting he was badly wounded in his left leg but refused to leave the battle until the pain and loss of blood caused him to faint. Arnold and his troops, chased by the British General Burgoyne, were forced to retreat into New York.

In recognition of Arnold's efforts, the Continental Congress promoted him to brigadier general in January 1776. As usual, there were those opposed to him. Unfriendly officers claimed that Arnold illegally took goods in Montreal, but an attempt to put him on trial failed.

During the fall of 1776 Arnold, commanding a small navy on Lake Champlain, battled a much larger British navy. The British wanted to recapture Fort Ticonderoga and to move south, hoping to join with another British army. If Burgoyne from the north and Howe from the south could control the Hudson River region they would have split New England from the rest of the states. This divide-and-conquer strategy was believed necessary for a British victory. Arnold was unable to defeat the British navy, but through clever and courageous maneuvers he delayed them and they were forced to withdraw to wait out the winter. Arnold had again risked his life in helping his country but, once again there were those who looked down on his efforts.

In February 1777, Arnold's pride was again insulted and his achievements unrewarded. The Continental Congress appointed five new major-generals, but Arnold was not among them. Because Connecticut already had two major-generals, a promotion for Arnold, also from Connecticut, might arouse jealousy in other states. George Washington was not consulted about the promotions and he was angered. Washington believed Arnold should have been promoted.

In a battle at Danbury, Connecticut, Arnold again showed great courage and leadership. The Continental Congress finally appointed him major-general but failed to give him proper seniority (priority over those of the same rank). At this point Benedict Arnold had had enough. He believed that, despite sacrificing much of his money, losing a happy family life, and risking his life to serve his country, political squabbles and lies had prevented him from receiving his proper reward. He sent a letter of resignation to the congress.

Congress also received a letter from Washington praising Arnold and requesting he be sent north to beat back Burgoyne who had recaptured Fort Ticonderoga and was moving toward Albany. Arnold asked that his resignation be suspended and moved north as directed.

Arnold had to serve under General Gates, and rivalry between them greatly distressed Arnold. Arnold's troops had been decisive in a battle at Freeman's Farm, but Gates did not give them the proper credit in his report of the battle. Arnold was outraged and, after a fierce argument with Gates, he asked to return to Washington's headquarters. Gates wanted Arnold to leave, but a petition was signed by many officers urging Arnold to stay. They knew of his outstanding ability in battle.

Further arguments with Gates occurred and Gates replaced Arnold with another general. As the important battle with Burgoyne was about to take place, Arnold was without a command. The battle was joined in October 1777 at Bemis Heights. Arnold could not stay on the sidelines. He leapt to his horse, and to the cheers of the troops, galloped into the fight. In the furious battle Arnold's performance was spectacular and the Americans defeated Burgoyne. Arnold narrowly missed being killed but was wounded again in the same leg that was hit at Quebec. Burgoyne later surrendered at Saratoga and claimed that Arnold's bravery was responsible for the American victory at Bemis Heights.

The defeat of Burgoyne was doubly important for the Americans. The British effort to split the colonies was again prevented. Also, the French, now believing the Americans had a good chance of winning the war, joined forces with the former colonies.

Arnold's wound was severe. Doctors recommended that his leg be amputated, but Arnold refused. Because of his crippling wounds, Arnold was never able to serve on the battlefield again.

During his long, painful recovery, Arnold went to Valley Forge in May 1778. There he signed an oath of allegiance that all officers were expected to sign. The oath said, in part, that Arnold owed his loyalty to the United States of America and not to the King of England and that he would support and defend the United States against England. Arnold willingly signed the oath. Soon afterward Washington appointed Arnold to the command of Philadelphia. If Arnold could have known what was to happen he probably would have refused the appointment. If Washington could have known what was to happen he probably would have never offered it.

Philadelphia, then capital of the United States, stirred with unrest brought on by the Revolution. There was friction and political jealousy between the Continental Congress, representing a central national authority, and the Pennsylvania Council, representing a strong state government. Not all the citizens of Philadelphia supported the Revolution. Many of them hoped the war could quickly be settled and that England, after making reforms, would still be the central government. There was also tension between the rich and poor. Wealthy Philadelphians often gave expensive parties that angered the poor citizens who had difficulty buying goods during the scarcity caused by wartime. As military commander of Philadelphia, Benedict Arnold stepped into the middle of these problems.

Among the wealthy in Philadelphia was the Shippen family. During the British occupation many parties and fancy balls had been given. Some Philadelphia citizens were invited. The beautiful Peggy Shippen was often invited to these social events and was frequently the center of attention. The British Major John André and Shippen became close friends during the occupation. The handsome, artistic, and charming André was perhaps even more popular than Shippen. When André and the British left, it seemed the elegant parties would end. Arnold, however, continued them.

Arnold lived in high style in Philadelphia. He met Peggy Shippen with whom he fell passionately in love. He persuaded her to marry him. In April 1779 they were wed. Like Arnold, she enjoyed wealth. His desire for money became stronger than ever.

Arnold's finances had suffered during the war. He often used his own money to supply his troops. In addition, he could not conduct his Connecticut business while dodging bullets on the battlefield. In Philadelphia he became friends with many wealthy businessmen, including Robert Morris, later called the financer of the Revolution. These men introduced Arnold to a variety of business activities.

Most of the businessmen did not think it wrong to make money during the Revolution. They often lost large amounts of money because of the conflict, so it seemed fair to make some when they could. Arnold's efforts to make money became the source of great controversy. One of his activities was the selling of supplies taken from captured ships. In one case he ordered army wagons to bring captured cargo to Philadelphia. He sold these goods (sugar, tea, glass, guns, etc.) and made a handsome profit. Such materials were difficult to obtain during wartime, so Arnold believed he was providing a service to the citizens. Not all agreed. His use of army wagons for private gain outraged those who heard of it.

One of those outraged was Joseph Reed, president of the Pennsylvania Council. He was suspicious of anyone who even seemed lukewarm in supporting the Revolution. He came to despise Arnold because of his expensive style of life and his association with wealthy businessmen. In addition, the Reed family did not like the Shippen family.

Reed was determined to discredit Benedict Arnold. So were others. Vicious rumors were spread. In one newspaper article it was claimed that Arnold had massacred Canadian villagers when retreating from Quebec. Such untrue stories furthered Arnold's sense that he was not being treated the way a hero was entitled to be.

In February 1779, as Arnold was on a trip to visit General Washington, the council published formal complaints against him, including his use of the wagons. Arnold had told the council that the truth of such charges should only be determined by the Continental Congress or General Washington. Reed and the council, believing they were the proper authority to hear the charges, were furious.

A committee of the Continental Congress, headed by William Paca, investigated the charges against Arnold and found only one, the wagon charge, to be justified. They recommended that military authorities decide what should be done about the charges. This further enraged the council. To prevent more conflict the congress decided to ignore the Paca report and recommend Arnold be court-martialed on some of the charges. Arnold was disgusted but wished a quick court-martial so that his innocence could be shown as soon as possible.

Washington agreed to May 1, 1779, as the date for the court-martial. Reed, feeling he didn't have enough evidence, wanted it delayed. Reed told Washington that unless the trial were delayed Pennsylvania would no longer provide transportation for the army. Washington felt he had no choice but to agree to postpone the trial. Arnold was again deeply hurt. Washington was one of the few men he trusted.

The court-martial was held in February 1780. Arnold was found not guilty on most of the charges, but his use of the wagons was determined to be improper. He was sentenced to be reprimanded by Washington. In his reprimand Washington wrote that Arnold's use of the wagons was reprehensible.

Arnold was crushed by this episode, but it did not directly lead him to treason. Almost a year earlier he had begun making secret contacts with the British.

Major André, now an aide to British General Clinton in New York, became Arnold's contact. Through a complicated system involving codes and the use of invisible ink, the bargaining went on. The British wanted to be sure Arnold could provide them a significant military advantage. Arnold wanted to be sure he would receive a large amount of money.

Arnold's wounds prevented him from taking command of an army which he could turn over to the British, but he did obtain the command of West Point, a fort on the Hudson River. If the British could hold that fort it would help them control the Hudson Valley.

They decided to reward Arnold if he would come over to their side. Some of Arnold's greatest military achievements had prevented the British from controlling the Hudson and splitting the colonies. Now, by his treason, he would be helping them gain the advantage his heroism had denied them.

It was arranged that André and Arnold would meet to discuss the plan. In the fall of 1780, André, aboard the British warship *Vulture*, sailed up the Hudson on his secret mission. Late at night he and Arnold met on the shore. Their talks went on through the night. With dawn approaching, the *Vulture* was forced to move down the river. André could not return to the ship. After hiding out for a time, it was decided André would have to return by land. He was disguised, and with secret papers in his boot, including a detailed map of West Point, he attempted to return to the British lines.

Unfortunately for André, he was captured by some American militiamen who intended to rob him. In the course of the robbery they found the secret papers and decided to turn them over to Washington. Washington was on his way to West Point for a meeting with Arnold. The general was stunned to discover that Arnold was planning treason.

Just before Washington was to arrive, Arnold discovered that André had been captured and that the treason plan was known by Washington. Arnold was able to escape from Washington and rowed down river to the safety of the *Vulture*.

André was not so lucky. Washington attempted to trade André for Arnold, but the British General Clinton, who was supposed to encourage Americans to come over to the British side, refused the trade. As a result, André was convicted of spying and hanged.

The British made good on their promise to pay Arnold a large sum of money, but the traitor was never respected by many of the British citizens. Arnold commanded a few naval expeditions for the British after which he and his wife moved to England. He died in England in 1801. The once honored military hero would be mainly remembered for his betrayal of his country.

The major sources for this story were:

Flexner, James T. *The Traitor and the Spy*. New York: Harcourt Brace, 1953.
Wallace, Willard M. *Traitorous Hero*. New York: Harper and Brothers, 1954.

ACTIVITIES FOR "FROM TRIUMPH TO TREASON"

Answer all questions on a separate sheet of paper.

Historical Understanding

Answer briefly:

1. What were three difficulties faced by the Continental Congress in preparing for the Revolution?
2. Why was control of the Hudson River important to the British?
3. What were two reasons that made Burgoyne's surrender at Saratoga important for the colonies?

Reviewing the Facts of the Case

Answer briefly:

1. Why was Arnold upset after the capture of Fort Ticonderoga?
2. What hardships did Arnold face in trying to capture Quebec?
3. Why didn't the Continental Congress promote Arnold in February 1777?
4. Why did many Philadelphians resent Arnold when he commanded the city?
5. For what offense was Arnold convicted?
6. What plans did Major André and Arnold discuss in the fall of 1780?

Analyzing Ethical Issues

There are a number of times in this story when people made ethical decisions. Ethical decisions are judgments of what is right or wrong, fair or unfair.

For example:

> The Continental Congress decided not to promote Arnold in spite of his heroism on Lake Champlain. They thought it would not be fair to allow Connecticut to have more generals than other states.

Find two other instances in which ethical decisions were made and explain the reasoning behind them.

Expressing Your Reasoning

1. Benedict Arnold was a man with great pride. He probably believed he was justified in betraying his country to help the British. What reasons would he be likely to give in trying to defend his treason? What would be the best arguments against his reasons?

2. Was Arnold wrong to use the army wagons for his personal gain? Why or why not?

3. Choose one of the two instances of ethical decision making you identified in the *Analyzing Ethical Issues* section above. In your judgment was the decision right or wrong? Write a paragraph explaining the reasons for your judgment.

4. *Seeking Additional Information.* In making decisions about such questions as those above, we often feel we need more information before we are satisfied with our judgments. Choose one of the above questions about which you would want more information than is presented in the story. What additional information would you like? Why would that information help you make a more satisfactory decision?

A Luxury We Can't Afford

THOMAS JEFFERSON AND SLAVERY

(*Courtesy of The University of Virginia Library*)

Isaac Jefferson: A Slave at Monticello

Thomas Jefferson stands out as one of the most distinguished leaders in American history. The list of his achievements in government is impressive. He was a delegate to the Virginia colonial legislature, author of the Declaration of Independence, governor of the State of Virginia, member of the U.S. House of Representatives, U.S. minister to France, secretary of state, and both vice president and president of the United States. As one of the founding fathers of the United States republic his ideas formed a cornerstone of U.S. democracy. His brilliant intellect has been admired from the colonial era to the present time. A more recent president, John F. Kennedy, honored him in an address given in 1962. Speaking before a group of Nobel Prize winners being honored at a White House dinner and reception, Kennedy said: "I think this is the most extraordinary collection of talent, of human knowledge, that has ever been gathered together at the White House, with the possible exception of when Thomas Jefferson dined alone."

To many it seemed odd that Jefferson, a patron saint of democracy and foe of tyranny, arose from a society based on slavery. Jefferson was in close contact with slavery from cradle to grave. His first memory was of being carried on a pillow by a slave. A slave carpenter made the coffin in which he was buried.

Though he regarded slavery as a "blot" and a "stain" upon America, Jefferson became one of the largest slaveholders of his time. Throughout his career he was troubled by the existence of slavery in America. A statement he made in 1820 reveals the continuing dilemma posed for him by slavery. In reference to slavery he said: "We have the wolf by the ears; and we can neither hold him, nor safely let him go. Justice is in one scale, and self-preservation in the other."

The story of Jefferson's struggle with slavery begins in Virginia. He was born there in 1743 and until his death was a member of its upper class. During the American Revolution when Jefferson said "my country" he meant Virginia. He was a Virginian before anything else, and he never ceased to be one. His roots went deep into Virginia soil. His ancestors had lived there for three generations before him. All of his formal education took place there. By age 40 he had spent less than a year outside the borders of Virginia.

In the year 1757, when Tom was 14, his father died. From his father Tom inherited an estate near Charlottesville including 30 slaves. This inheritance made Tom a member of the Virginia aristocracy.

Tom's father had wanted his son to be well schooled. His dying instruction was that the boy receive a thorough classical education. Tom later said that he was more grateful for this than all the privileges his father placed within his reach. From private tutors he learned Greek and Latin. Later he attended the College of William and Mary in Williamsburg, the colonial capital. He loved books as much as he hated laziness and applied himself eagerly to his studies. After college he became a law student in Williamsburg at the age of 19. In 1765 Thomas Jefferson officially became a lawyer. His father's wish had been satisfied. The boy was well schooled and refined of manners. Socially, in all respects, he was considered a gentleman.

Before he was to step on the public stage, Jefferson's education had made him a student of the *Enlightenment*. Beginning in Europe, the Enlightenment was a cluster of ideas closely tied to human freedom. Enlightenment thinkers believed that mankind was emerging from the shackles of darkness. In their view the time had come for people to be forward-looking and free of old superstitions and myths.

Enlightenment philosophers believed that the path of reason and science would lead to discovery of natural laws that governed the universe. Out of this natural law doctrine came the political idea of natural rights. One such right that absorbed Jefferson was liberty. To Jefferson liberty meant freedom from both tyranny and oppression.

Two years after he began the practice of law, Thomas Jefferson took the case, without fee, of Samuel Howell. Both Howell's mother and grandmother had been slaves who were freed. Howell sued for freedom from the master to whom he had been sold before his mother received her freedom.

Jefferson argued that Virginia law did not extend slavery to the offspring of slaves who had been set free. His arguments in court went beyond the laws of Virginia. He invoked the "law of nature." Under that law, he said, "We are all born free." The Virginia court ruled against him. Such Enlightenment ideas carried no weight with a practical-minded judge in a slaveowning society. Slaves were considered essential to the cheap production of the cotton and tobacco crops of Virginia plantations.

Following a brief period of practicing law, Jefferson entered the political arena. In 1769 the *freeholders* (white landowners) of Albermarle County met in the Charlottesville courthouse to elect their representative to the Virginia House of Burgesses. They chose as their burgess 25-year-old Thomas Jefferson. While a burgess, Jefferson regarded himself a loyal subject of the Crown. He drank toasts to the king and royal governor. From the beginning, however, he defended colonial rights against the Crown, strongly opposing the taxes England placed on the colony.

Just when colonial rights were becoming a major issue in 1772, Jefferson decided to settle down. He had married Martha Skelton and had for several years been building a house. For the time being he put public affairs aside and tended to personal matters.

He arranged for the leveling of the little mountain on the estate he inherited from his father. He translated "little mountain" into Italian. Monticello became the name of the plantation to which Jefferson devoted a lifetime of building. His house at Monticello is today a famous architectural monument. To Jefferson, always a domestic man, it was simply his home and the center of his life. His heart was on his mountain top. There he found privacy and the peace of family life.

Upon the death of his father-in-law, two years after Jefferson married, his wealth doubled. Included in his wife's inheritance were 135 slaves. This brought the total of his slaves at Monticello to 185.

Compared to most slaveholders, Jefferson was a kind master. A French nobleman visiting Monticello reported that Jefferson's slaves were nourished, clothed, and treated as well as white servants could be. Jefferson rewarded hard work with extra rations of food and time off for slaves to work their own gardens. He once described Monticello as a place "where all is peace and harmony, where we love and are loved by every object we see."

Jefferson never personally applied the lash, and he directed that overseers whip slaves only in extreme cases. He always preferred to sell disobedient slaves rather than to flog them. When selling such slaves, unlike other masters, Jefferson tried to dispose of families as a unit. He tried not to separate parents and children, husbands and wives.

In addition to growing tobacco and cotton Jefferson had nails manufactured at Monticello. They were sold in Richmond for a handsome profit. The slave boys who worked in the naillery shared in this prosperity. They received a pound of meat a week, a dozen herrings, a quart of molasses, and a peck of meal. Those who turned out the most nails were rewarded with a suit of red or blue cloth. Not all slaves at Monticello were content, however. When the Revolutionary War broke out, about thirty of Jefferson's slaves escaped from Monticello and fought with the British army.

Soon after Jefferson settled down at Monticello the political pot in the colonies began to simmer. The growing conflict between colonies and Crown took a radical shift when Virginia suggested a meeting in Philadelphia of the various colonies to draft a joint protest. This meeting marks the birth of the Continental Congress. In 1775 Virginians sent Jefferson as one of their delegates to the congress in Philadelphia. From this date onward Jefferson's story becomes a key part of the history of the republic. Political events snatched him from his happiness as husband and father.

The Virginia delegates were instructed to propose to congress that the united colonies be declared free and independent states. Jefferson had come to support this proposal because of recent acts of Parliament. In his view trade with all parts of the world was a natural right of the colonies. The acts of Parliament that restricted colonial trade were void, he wrote, because "the British Parliament has no right to exercise authority over us."

In response to the Virginia proposal, congress appointed a committee to prepare a declaration. The committee comprised John Adams of Massachusetts, Benjamin Franklin of Pennsylvania, and Thomas Jefferson of Virginia. Those meeting in Philadelphia considered the document about to be written an important one, but nobody then knew it would become immortal.

Jefferson was asked to draft the declaration. What he wrote was presented to the whole congress on June 28, 1776. Members of the congress debated the document before voting on it. According to the rules, the vote had to be unanimous for the resolution to be adopted. Several changes were made before the final vote was taken. The most heated conflict occurred in the debate over Jefferson's words about slavery. The delegates from South Carolina and Georgia objected to the passage in Jefferson's draft that condemned King George for the slave trade. His passage read:

> He [King George III] has waged cruel war against human nature itself, violating its most sacred rights of life and liberty in the persons of a distant people who never offended him, captivating and carrying them into slavery in another hemisphere or to incur miserable death in their transportation thither. This piratical warfare . . . is the warfare of the Christian King of Great Britain.

Scene 7 of the play by Peter Stone and Sherman Edwards entitled *1776* presents a dramatic account of the debate over this passage by members of the Continental Congress. The characters in this part of the play are:

Edward Rutledge: Delegate from South Carolina
John Hancock: President of the Continental Congress
Charles Thompson: Secretary of the Continental Congress
Thomas Jefferson: Delegate from Virginia
John Adams: Delegate from Massachusetts
Stephen Hopkins: Delegate from Rhode Island
Benjamin Franklin: Delegate from Pennsylvania

HANCOCK: If there are no more changes, then, I can assume that the report of the Declaration Committee has been ——

RUTLEDGE (*deliberately*):   Just a moment, Mr. President.

FRANKLIN (*to John*):   Look out.

RUTLEDGE: I wonder if we could prevail upon Mr. Thompson to read again a small portion of Mr. Jefferson's Declaration— the one beginning "He has waged cruel war—"?

HANCOCK: Mr. Thompson?

THOMPSON (*reading back rapidly to himself*):   ". . . He has affected . . . He has combined . . . He has abdicated . . . He has plundered . . . He has constrained . . . He has excited . . . He has incited . . . He has waged cruel war! Ah. (*He looks up.*) Here it is. (*He clears his throat and reads.*) "He had waged cruel war against human nature itself, in the persons of a distant people who never offended him, captivating and carrying them into slavery in another hemisphere. Determined to keep open a market where men should be bought and sold, he has prostituted——

RUTLEDGE: That will suffice, Mr. Thompson, I thank you. Mr. Jefferson, I can't quite make out what it is you're talkin' about.

JEFFERSON: Slavery, Mr. Rutledge.

RUTLEDGE: Ah, yes. You're referrin' to us as slaves of the King.

JEFFERSON: No sir, I'm referring to our slaves. Black slaves.

RUTLEDGE: Ah, Black slaves. Why didn't you say so, sir? Were you tryin' to hide your meanin'?

JEFFERSON: No, sir.

RUTLEDGE: Just another literary license, then?

JEFFERSON: If you like.

RUTLEDGE: I don't like at all, Mr. Jefferson. To us in South Carolina, black slavery is our peculiar institution and a cherished way of life.

JEFFERSON: Nevertheless, we must abolish it. Nothing is more certainly written in the Book of Fate than that this people shall be free.

RUTLEDGE: I am not concerned with the Book of Fate right now, sir. I am more concerned with what's written in your little paper there.

JOHN [ADAMS]: That "little paper there" deals with freedom for Americans!

RUTLEDGE: Oh, really! Mr. Adams is now callin' our black slaves Americans. Are-they-now?

JOHN: They are! They're people and they're here—if there is any other requirement, I've never heard of it.

RUTLEDGE: They are here, yes, but they are not people, sir, they are property.

JEFFERSON: No, sir! They are people who are being treated as property. I tell you the rights of human nature are deeply wounded by this infamous practice!

RUTLEDGE (*shouting*): Then see to your own wounds, Mr. Jefferson, for you are a—practitioner—are you not? (*A pause. Rutledge has found the mark.*)

JEFFERSON: I have already resolved to release my slaves.

RUTLEDGE: Then I'm sorry, for you have also resolved the ruination of your personal economy.

JOHN: Economy. Always economy. There's more to this than a filthy purse string, Rutledge. It's an offense against man and God.

HOPKINS: It's a stinking business, Mr. Rutledge—a stinking business.

RUTLEDGE: Is it really, Mr. Hopkins? Then what's that I smell floatin' down from the North—could it be the aroma of hypocrisy? For who holds the other end of that filthy purse-string, Mr. Adams? (*To everyone*) Our northern brethren are feelin' a bit tender toward our slaves. They don't keep slaves, no-o, but they're willin', for the shillin'—(*rubbing his thumb and forefinger together*)—or haven't y'heard, Mr. Adams? Clink! Clink! . . .

. . .

Gentlemen! You mustn't think our northern friends merely see our slaves as figures on a ledger. Oh no, sir! They see them as figures on the block! Notice the faces at the auctions, gentlemen—white faces on the African wharves—New England faces, seafaring faces: "Put them in the ships, cram them in the ships, stuff them in the ships!" Hurry gentlemen, let the auction begin! . . .

. . .

Mr. Adams, I give you a toast! Hail, Boston! Hail, Charleston! Who stinketh the most?!?!? (*He turns and walks straight out of the Chamber. Hewes of North Carolina follows, and Hall of Georgia is right behind them. Others leave the chamber. Only Franklin, Jefferson, Hancock, and Thompson remain.*)

FRANKLIN: We've no other choice, John. This slavery clause has to go.

JOHN: Franklin, what are y'saying?

FRANKLIN: It's a luxury we can't afford.

JOHN: A luxury? A half-million souls in chains, and Dr. Franklin calls it a luxury! Maybe you should have walked out with the South!

FRANKLIN: You forget yourself, sir! I founded the first anti-slavery society on this continent.

JOHN: Don't wave your credentials at me! Perhaps it's time you had them renewed!

FRANKLIN (*angrily*): The issue here is independence! Maybe you've lost sight of that fact, but I have not! How dare you jeopardize our cause when we've come so far? These men, no matter how much we disagree with them, are not ribbon clerks to be ordered about; they're proud, accomplished men, the cream of their colonies—and whether you like it or not, they and the people they represent will be part of the new country you'd hope to create! Either start learning how to live with them or pack up and go home—but in any case, stop acting like a Boston fishwife!

Adams was finally persuaded that the antislavery passage in the Declaration should be removed. Jefferson reluctantly agreed to delete the passage from his draft. With it remaining, there could be no unanimous vote for independence. The passage removed, the Declaration of Independence was unanimously adopted by the delegates meeting in Philadelphia.

For Thomas Jefferson, the main issue in the debate over the Declaration had not been slavery. Though Jefferson opposed slavery, his main concern was independence from England and new principles of government for the colonies. Deleting the slavery passage from the Declaration, he thought, was a small price to pay for his broader goals. Once independence was achieved the slavery issue could be raised again. Jefferson would repeatedly have to decide what to do about slavery in light of his most memorable words from the Declaration: "We hold these truths to be self-evident: that all men are created equal; that they are endowed by their creator with certain unalienable rights; that among these are life, liberty, and the pursuit of happiness."

Jefferson did not forget that he had offered a creed for himself and the new republic. The challenge for him would now be to make this creed a living reality. He went back home to Virginia to take a major hand in the drafting of a new constitution and new laws for his native state. His return to the national scene would await the building of the State of Virginia as a proving ground for the major new social and political order.

A major issue for the new order was slavery. Jefferson was convinced that slavery was an intolerable wrong. Yet, he thought it would be better to send former slaves, once freed, out of the country where they could set up a colony of their own. After emancipation he believed blacks and whites would be unable to live in peace under the same government. Deep-seated prejudices ingrained in whites and the memory of injuries suffered by blacks would produce violent uprisings.

Upon his return to Virginia, Jefferson tried to translate his hatred of slavery into state law. In his 1776 draft of a new state constitution he introduced a clause prohibiting future importation of slaves. He later proposed freedom for the children of all Virginia slaves born after 1800. Freedom, he said, was "the birthright of all men regardless of their color or condition." His fellow Virginians did not share his views on freedom for slaves. They rejected both of his proposals.

As a result of repeated rebuffs, it became clear to Jefferson that the time had not arrived for the government to abolish slavery. Nonetheless, he could still act personally to free his own slaves. A sense of guilt beset him.

Setting his own slaves free posed several obstacles for Jefferson. Since he was often burdened by debt, he hired out some of his slaves to raise money. Outright selling of his slaves would have been the quickest way to raise cash to pay his creditors, but to do so would have deprived him of the labor force upon which his income depended and would have had an adverse effect on his comfortable style of living. Without slaves, a Virginia plantation like Monticello could not function.

Another obstacle to freeing his own slaves was the law of Virginia. Under Virginia law, a master who took a slave to the county court to gain his or her release had to certify that the slave had a skill and a place to use it. It was unlawful to free a slave without first providing for his or her support. This would have been extremely difficult for Jefferson, because he owned so many slaves. Colonial Virginia was organized around the great plantations. There was no place, off the plantation, for large numbers of freed slaves to settle. Also, freed slaves were not welcome in other states, several of which excluded their entry by law.

Despite these obstacles, *abolitionists* (those favoring freedom for slaves) urged Jefferson to set an example by freeing his own slaves. They urged the patriarch of Monticello to put the full weight of his immense prestige on the side of the antislavery movement. Jefferson, they said, was in a position to set an example that would lead other Virginia planters to free their slaves.

The famed black mathematician Benjamin Banneker claimed that Jefferson was violating his own principles by holding blacks as slaves. In a letter to Jefferson, Banneker asked him to reconcile his "created equal" phrase from the Declaration with his practice of "detaining by fraud and violence so numerous a part of my brethren, under groaning captivity."

Jefferson came to take the position that emancipation was an idea whose time had not yet come. He thought it would be a mistake to try to hasten its coming. His aim was gradually to place slavery in the course of ultimate extinction. He was awaiting the "ripening" of public opinion. He believed a premature effort against slavery would result in an irreversible setback. He did not want to get so far in advance of public opinion that he lost his political followers. A successful reformer, he thought, ought not rush in where revolutionaries might fear to tread. Overeager zealots might set the cause back.

Thomas Jefferson died on July 4, 1826, without freeing most of his slaves. At the time of his death he had one of the largest holdings of slaves in Virginia. If Jefferson had freed his slaves, he would have jeopardized his political career. He would not have succeeded in doing the things in which he took the greatest pride. It is most unlikely that he would have become president of the United States. Not until 1860 was a man actively opposed to the spread of slavery elected to that high office.

The major sources for this story were:

David, D. B. *Was Thomas Jefferson an Authentic Enemy of Slavery?* Oxford, England: Oxford University Press, 1970.

Malone, Dumas. *Jefferson the Virginian*. Boston: Little, Brown, 1948.

Miller, John C. *The Wolf by the Ears*. New York: The Free Press, 1977.

Stone, Peter, and Edwards, Sherman. *1776*. New York: Viking Press, 1964 (play excerpts from pp. 112–121).

ACTIVITIES FOR "A LUXURY WE CAN'T AFFORD"

Answer all questions on a separate sheet of paper.

Historical Understanding

Answer briefly:

1. How did the Enlightenment influence Jefferson's view of slavery?

2. What did Jefferson mean when he said: "We have the wolf by the ears; and we can neither hold him, nor safely let him go"?

3. For what purpose did the First Continental Congress meet?

4. Why was the antislavery passage deleted from the draft of the Declaration of Independence?

5. In what ways did some New Englanders benefit from slavery?

Reviewing the Facts of the Case

Answer briefly:

1. State two ways that slaves at Monticello were treated differently from slaves on most other plantations.

2. For what reasons did Jefferson believe that freed blacks and whites could not live peacefully together in the United States?

3. Why were Jefferson's antislavery proposals rejected by Virginia lawmakers?

4. What economic effect would freeing his slaves have had on Jefferson?

5. What did Virginia law require of masters who wished to free their slaves?

Analyzing Ethical Issues

Equality is a value concerning whether people should be treated in the same way. There are places in this story where the value of equality conflicts with other values:

PROPERTY: A value concerning what people should be allowed to own and how they should be allowed to use it.

AUTHORITY: A value concerning what rules or people should be obeyed and the consequences for disobedience.

Indicate two places in the story where the value of equality is in conflict with one of these values—property and authority. First identify the value that conflicts with equality. Then briefly identify the incident in the story where the conflict occurs, as illustrated in the following example:

VALUE CONFLICT   WHERE THE CONFLICT OCCURS
Equality (for slaves) versus   *Benjamin Franklin had to de-*
liberty (for the colonies).   *cide whether or not to delete*
                                   the antislavery passage from the
                                   Declaration.

Expressing Your Reasoning

1. Should Thomas Jefferson have freed his slaves? Why or why not?

2. Some have argued that it might be wrong to own slaves in the twentieth century, but that during the eighteenth century it was morally acceptable. Can an action be right at one time and wrong at another? Explain your thinking.

3. For each situation below specify a basis for comparison and explain whether you think the people involved were treated equally:

SITUATION

British subjects in England were represented by elected representatives in Parliament, but colonists were not.

BASIS FOR COMPARISON

If the basis for comparing the two groups is opportunity to influence legislation, then the colonists were being treated unequally because they had no direct voice in the legislature.

a. Virginia was allowed more representatives in Congress than Rhode Island. (citizens of Virginia/citizens of Rhode Island)
b. Jefferson gave special bonuses to those slaves who produced the most nails at the Monticello naillery. (slaves producing more nails/slaves producing fewer nails)
c. Thomas Jefferson's inheritance was greater than that of his sister. (Thomas/his sister)

Write a short position paper answering the question: Does *equal* treatment of people require that they receive *identical* treatment? Refer to the situations above, as well as other examples, in what you write.

4. *Seeking Additional Information.* In making decisions about such questions as those above we often feel we need more information before we are satisfied with our judgments. Choose one of the above questions about which you would want more information than is presented in the story. What additional information would you like? Why would that information help you make a more satisfactory decision?

PART 2

The New Nation
(1777–1850)

The Desperate Debtors

SHAYS' REBELLION

Shays' Rebellion, January 1787, Springfield, Massachusetts

As a result of the Revolution, Americans were freed from the hated British taxes. While the war brought freedom, it did not produce a united United States. Most of the former colonists probably thought of themselves first as citizens of particular states, and second as citizens of a new American nation.

The Articles of Confederation established a weak central government. Could this new government solve the problems that the new nation would face? Each of the former colonies had new state governments. Could these governments deal effectively with their own problems and command the loyalty of their citizens? These were major political questions of the time.

There were economic as well as political problems. The war had been expensive. States had borrowed money to pay their soldiers and to buy supplies. Now these debts had to be repaid. The new state governments also needed money to pay their operating expenses. To raise money the states had to tax their citizens. Many citizens were poor and in debt and found it difficult to pay taxes and repay debts.

In Massachusetts these political and economic problems formed the background for a series of events which became known as Shays' Rebellion. Many feared these events would spell doom for the attempt to form a new nation.

The war had been especially costly for Massachusetts and the state was deeply in debt. Many citizens were also in financial trouble and had difficulty paying their taxes. In eastern Massachusetts, once wealthy merchants who had relied on the profitable West Indies trade, were losing money. The British still controlled the islands and were preventing American ships from trading there.

In western Massachusetts, farmers were also in financial trouble. Money was in short supply and prices for farm products were low. Farmers often found they could barely survive. Also, farmers had borrowed money to buy their land and supplies. These loans had to be repaid and state taxes had to be paid. Poor farmers could often do neither.

When debtors were unable to repay loans, their *creditors* (the people to whom they owed money) could take them to court. Debtors were taken to the Court of Common Pleas where the judges decided what was to happen. Sometimes a farmer's goods would be taken and sold at auction to get money to pay the creditors. Because people in the area had little money, a farmer's goods often sold for much less than they had originally cost. The farmer's land could also be taken as part of the debt repayment. Furthermore, judges could send the farmer to jail until someone repaid his loan. Hundreds of debt-ridden farmers were unable to pay. In 1785, the Court of Common Pleas heard over 800 cases from Hampshire County alone.

The courts had been established by law, but many farmers wanted the laws changed. Some wanted the courts to be closed until economic conditions improved. Others wanted the state to print paper money and pass a law requiring creditors to accept that money. Many debts had to be paid in *specie* (gold or silver currency) but there was very little specie available. Many farmers believed that legalized paper money would solve their problems.

The farmers had other complaints. They felt the costs of government were too high. For example, they believed the governor's salary should be cut. They also objected to the high fees that lawyers were allowed to charge. Throughout the early 1780s, farmers met in county conventions and drew up petitions to the legislature asking that the laws be changed.

The new state government made some changes but not enough to ease the economic problems of the farmers. Governor James Bowdoin and other officials were distressed by the behavior of some of the westerners. It was one thing to request peacefully that laws be changed, but some farmers were taking the law into their own hands. As early as 1782, a mob of angry farmers had managed to close a session of the Court of Common Pleas in Berkshire County.

The legislature was unwilling to pass a paper money law. Such a law had been passed in Rhode Island but it had bad effects. Many merchants distrusted the new money and refused to accept it as payment. These merchants often left Rhode Island. The law had not solved the financial problems there.

More and more sessions of court were closed down by protesting farmers. One of the early leaders of the farmers, Samuel Ely, supposedly urged his men to get clubs and knock the wigs off the judges' heads. Many of the farmers had fought in the Revolution but now believed their own government, rather than the British, was against them. Such war veterans as Luke Day and Daniel Shays began organizing farmers to continue shutting down the courts.

Government officials were getting nervous. In New Hampshire, they heard that a mob of armed farmers had surrounded the legislature and only left when the state guard was called out. Massachusetts was struggling to solve its financial problems, and now it seemed there was the beginning of an armed rebellion.

Sam Adams, now a state senator, was determined to treat the rebellious farmers harshly. Adams had been a leader in urging the Revolution against England, but he did not think the farmers had a right to rebel against their own elected government. He worked to get a law passed that would punish the farmers but was unable to get enough votes for its passage.

The western farmers heard rumors about the proposed harsh laws. Some had heard the death penalty was going to be the punishment for closing down the courts. In the fall of 1786, a letter was sent to various western towns. The letter said that the legislature was going to enact the death penalty and urged farmers to organize, get weapons, select officers, and "be ready to turn out at a minute's warning." It was signed by Daniel Shays, although he later said he had not put his name to the letter.

Government officials discovered a copy of the letter. Now it seemed certain that an armed rebellion was coming. The farmers were organizing into groups of minutemen, and Daniel Shays must have been their leader. Now, Sam Adams was able to get enough votes. The Riot Act was passed. According to this law, the local sheriff could order rebel farmers to leave the area. If they refused to leave within one hour, they could be arrested, lose their property, and be physically punished. Another law permitted government officials to put in jail anyone they believed was harmful to the state.

In addition to the strict laws, a peace offering was passed. According to this law, the Indemnity Act, no rebels would be punished if they signed an oath of loyalty to the state and immediately stopped trying to shut down the courts.

News of the strict laws quickly reached the farmers, but the Indemnity Act had not gotten much publicity. A few days after its passage, a group of farmers shut down the court at Worcester. The sheriff had read the Riot Act but it did not move the farmers. Later officials captured a number of the rebel farmers and jailed them.

The news upset Daniel Shays. The government clearly meant to put down the farmers and not respond to their financial plight. It seemed the farmers would have to continue with their rebellion even more vigorously. But should Shays lead them? If he took the loyalty oath he might avoid punishment and possibly death. However, one of his advisors told him that the Indemnity Act would not apply to him because he was considered to be the leader of the rebels. There was no way of knowing for sure. General Rufus Putnam, an old friend of Shays and his commanding officer during the Revolution, urged him to seek a pardon from the government. Shays decided against it.

News of the capture of some farmers and the strict new laws led Shays to sign a letter to be sent to the western towns. The letter began, "The seeds of war are now sown." It ended with an appeal for the towns to supply men and provisions for the continued struggle with the government. Massachusetts was divided between those who supported the farmers and those who supported the government.

News of the conflict in Massachusetts spread throughout the states. George Washington feared for the security of the new nation. He said, if the farmers had genuine complaints then the government should try to make changes, but government should not be overthrown. Washington wrote: "If they have real grievances, redress them, if possible; or acknowledge the justice of them, and your inability to do it at the moment. If they have not, employ the force of government against them at once."

Thomas Jefferson held a different view. He was in Paris at the time of the rebellion, but he later wrote: "I hold it that a little rebellion now and then is a good thing, and as necessary in the political world as storms in the physical. . . . It is medicine necessary for the sound health of government."

Shays became determined to give the government a strong dose of medicine. In January 1787, the Massachusetts government sent General Benjamin Lincoln with a force of about 4,000 men to put down the rebels. Shays knew the farmers needed more weapons and ammunition if they had to do battle with Lincoln. At Springfield there was a federal arsenal that held guns and ammunition. It was decided to march on the arsenal before Lincoln could get there.

It seems that Shays believed he could take the arsenal without bloodshed. Many of the 900 troops guarding the arsenal knew Shays and his men, so it was unlikely they would fire on them. Also, the commander of the arsenal troops had avoided using force in a previous encounter.

On January 25, Shays and over one thousand men marched to the front of the arensal. The commander ordered his men to fire two warning shots over the heads of the farmers. The shots were fired to no effect. Shays' men marched forward and the commander ordered his men to fire at the farmers. They obeyed the order. Four of Shays' men were killed and the rest broke ranks and ran. Shays' army did not fire a single shot. They retreated in disarray.

General Lincoln's troops reached the area and pursued Shays' retreating men. After marching through a freezing, snowy night, Lincoln's men surprised Shays' at Petersham. Many of Shays' men surrendered. Shays and others escaped into Vermont.

In the following months there were many skirmishes as the government troops tried to round up rebel farmers still at large. In the meantime, Governor Bowdoin and other government officials had to decide what to do with the captured rebels. Sam Adams believed that they should be hanged. Others wanted less severe punishment. Still others favored the granting of a general pardon. It was agreed that something should be done to show that government must be obeyed. It was decided that a few of the rebels should be hanged and the rest pardoned.

The decision to hang a few rebels was not popular. When John Hancock was elected governor and took office in June, he granted a general pardon. A year later, Daniel Shays formally received his pardon.

During the trouble in Massachusetts the central government under the Articles of Confederation had been unable to provide help. The weakness of the government in this case was one factor that led to the formation of a stronger central government, the one established by the Constitution.

The major sources for this story were:

Starkey, Marion L. *A Little Rebellion*. New York: Alfred A. Knopf, 1955.

Taylor, Robert J. *Western Massachusetts in the Revolution*. Providence, R.I.: Brown University Press, 1954.

ACTIVITIES FOR "THE DESPERATE DEBTORS"

Answer all questions on a separate piece of paper.

Historical Understanding

Answer briefly:

1. What were three reasons for the financial troubles faced by many Massachusetts citizens?

2. Why were people throughout the United States concerned about the turmoil in Massachusetts?

3. In what ways did Thomas Jefferson and George Washington differ in their opinions about Shays' Rebellion?

Reviewing the Facts of the Case

Answer briefly:

1. What was the Court of Common Pleas?

2. What could happen to farmers who did not pay their debts?

3. What changes in the laws did the farmers want?

4. What was the Riot Act? What was the Indemnity Act?

5. What did Shays urge people to do in his letter to the western towns?

Analyzing Ethical Issues

There is agreement on the answer to some questions. For other questions there is disagreement about the answer. We call these questions issues. Issues can be categorized as factual or ethical. A factual issue asks whether something is true or false, accurate or inaccurate. An ethical issue asks whether something is right or wrong, fair or unfair. Factual issues ask what *is*; ethical issues ask what *ought* to be.

For each of the following questions decide whether the issue is factual or ethical, as illustrated in this example.

Would Daniel Shays have been executed if he had surrendered and sought a pardon?   *Factual.*

Should the legislature have passed a paper money bill?   *Ethical.*

1. Could Shays' men have taken control of the arsenal?

2. Could the Massachusetts government have afforded to make the changes the farmers wanted?

3. Should John Hancock have followed Sam Adams' advice about the death penalty?

4. Would the rebellion have ended if Shays had followed Putnam's advice and sought a pardon?

5. Was it right for Shays to send the letter?

Think back over the story and identify and write down two factual questions and two ethical questions related to the Shays Rebellion.

Expressing Your Reasoning

1. General Rufus Putnam urged Shays to seek a pardon from the government. What would be the best reason for him to seek a pardon? What would be the best reason for him *not* to seek a pardon? Should Daniel Shays have sought the pardon? Why or why not?

2. Sam Adams believed the colonists were right in rebelling against England but the farmers of Massachusetts were wrong in rebelling against the state. Do you agree with Adams? Why or why not? Write a paragraph expressing your point of view.

3. *Seeking Additional Information.* In making decisions about such questions as those above, we often feel we need more information before we are satisfied with our judgments. Choose one of the above questions about which you would want more information than is presented in the story. What additional information would you like? Why would that information help you make a more satisfactory decision?

The Price of Free Speech

ALIEN AND SEDITION ACTS

John Adams

(*State Historical Society of Wisconsin*)

John Adams

By 1788 enough states had approved the Constitution so that the new federal government could begin. Not everyone favored the Constitution and debates within each state had been intense. Now there was a new government—at least on paper. What kind of government would it be in practice? Would the federal government be strong enough to avoid past problems? Would the states obey the authority of the central government? Could the new nation be protected from possible foreign dangers? No one knew the answers to these questions. The new nation was yet to be shaped by experience.

As first president, war-hero George Washington was able to help get the new government underway. By the end of his time in office, serious problems had developed. These problems were to haunt the next president, John Adams. One of these problems was the bitter differences between political parties. The Constitution had not provided for the existence of political parties, but their growth had a powerful effect on the new nation.

One of the parties was called the Federalists; the other, Republicans. The parties reflected general disagreements among people. At times the two parties seemed to disagree about everything.

Generally, the Federalists wanted a strong national government, friendly relations with England, and an economy built on manufacturing. The Federalists were most powerful in the northeastern states.

On the other hand, the Republicans wanted greater limits on the power of the federal government. They favored friendly relations with France and an economy based on agriculture. Republicans were strongest in the middle and southern states.

Federalists believed that the wealthy upper classes should control the government; Republicans believed the common people should have the biggest influence. The Republicans often feared that the Federalists wanted to make the new nation a monarchy as in England. A leading Federalist was Alexander Hamilton. A leading Republican was Thomas Jefferson.

Differences between the parties became severe in the 1790s. During that time problems with foreign nations threatened the safety of the new nation.

France had helped the colonies win their independence from England. After the Revolution, France was admired by most Americans. Then, beginning in 1789, France went through a series of violent revolutions. News of these events, a reign of terror in France, and French invasions of other European countries affected American thinking. Some people, mainly Republicans, were delighted that France had overthrown its king and was now attacking other monarchies. Others, mainly Federalists, feared the French example would stimulate violence in the United States.

Tensions between the political parties increased when England and France went to war. According to a treaty signed in 1778, the United States had agreed to defend the French West Indies if they were threatened during wartime. George Washington believed the revolutions in France had nullified the treaty. He also did not want the young United States to become involved in a war. In 1793, he proclaimed that the United States would be neutral—would not take sides—in the European conflict.

French leaders were angered by this. They believed the United States had violated its treaty agreement. Also, they feared the United States was becoming too friendly with England and might even form an alliance. To get back at the United States, the French navy began attacking U.S. merchant ships, taking their cargo and often injuring their sailors. In 1795 about three hundred U.S. ships were captured.

When Federalist John Adams became president in 1796, anti-French feelings ran high among the members of his party. Republicans thought there was little danger to the United States, though many Federalists expected a full-scale war. Adams believed the French naval actions were, in effect, a declaration of war. It was, however a half-war: "She is at war with us, but we are not at war with her."

Adams wanted to avoid a war with France. In 1797 he sent three ambassadors to negotiate with the French government. The French foreign minister sent his agents, later known as X, Y, and Z, to talk with the ambassadors. The agents said the government would not begin to negotiate unless the U.S. government first paid a bribe of $250,000 and gave France a multimillion dollar loan. The Americans refused and no peace talks were held.

When the news of the XYZ affair reached the United States, most people were shocked and offended. When John Marshall, one of the ambassadors, returned, he was treated as a hero for turning down the French insults. A slogan of the day was: "Millions for defense, but not a cent for tribute." Americans were unwilling to pay bribes to the French.

Hatred and fear of the French became common, particularly among Federalists. Many believed the French had secret agents in the United States who were plotting a revolution. Vice-President Thomas Jefferson, generally friendly toward France, was regarded as one of the

Federalists' enemies. Some newspapers printed a letter that they claimed had been written by Jefferson. The author of the letter said he hoped the supporters of France would take power in the United States.

Arguments between supporters of the Federalists and Republicans were common. Brawls took place in the streets. Newspapers took sides, some vigorously supporting the Adams administration, others vigorously opposing it.

Political party differences seemed to surround everything. A Federalist newspaper reported a bank robbery. In the article the robber was identified as a Republican. Even disease became political. Epidemics of yellow fever were common in Philadelphia during the summer months. In one instance, Republicans claimed the disease was carried in British ships while Federalists claimed it was spread by French ships.

The French continued to attack U.S. shipping, sometimes even in sight of the United States shoreline. To many it seemed war was inevitable. Some Federalists urged Adams to declare war. Adams made many speeches attacking the French but did not ask for a declaration of war. Instead, he urged Congress to pass laws for defense.

In spite of Republican opposition, the Federalist-dominated Congress passed many defense laws. A navy was to be built, an army raised, and new taxes were set to pay for them. George Washington came out of retirement to head the new army. Alexander Hamilton was to be his second-in-command.

In addition to these actions, Congress passed a series of laws known as the Alien and Sedition Acts. Among other things, the Alien Acts gave the president the power to order out of the country any foreigners "he shall judge dangerous to the peace and safety of the United States." The Alien Acts also made it more difficult for foreigners to become citizens. According to the new law a person had to live in the United States for 14 years before becoming eligible for citizenship. Prior to this, a person had to live in the country for only 5 years.

Republicans opposed the Alien Acts partly because they increased the president's power. Some of them still feared the Federalists were trying to establish a monarchy.

Republicans were most outraged by the passage of the Sedition Act, which prohibited statements bringing the government into contempt or opposing its laws. According to the Sedition Act it was a crime for any person to print or say anything "false, scandalous or malicious" against the president or members of Congress. The law was to be in effect from July 1778 to March 1801.

Faced with a possible war in France, the Federalists wanted to avoid a possible uprising in the United States. They believed the new law would help them. One Federalist wrote: "The poor . . . with many of the ignorant, are easily formed into a revolutionary corps in every country." Another writer said it would not take many people to start trouble: "One frantic madman may bawl FIRE! at midnight, and disturb the peace and fears of a whole city—one furious French supporter could alarm a whole country with ridiculous fears of the government. The alarm is caught by the weak, and spread by the foolish."

Republicans opposed the Sedition law, claiming it violated the First Amendment of the Constitution. The First Amendment said that government could not interfere with the freedoms of speech and press. Once again the Republicans feared the government was taking on too much power. They also believed the Federalists were trying to destroy the Republican party. All the federal judges were Federalists and it was suspected they would probably use the laws only against Republican writers and speakers.

Federalists argued that free speech did not mean total freedom. There had to be limits. One Federalist said it would be foolish to "complain against laws made for punishing assault and murder as restraints upon the freedom of men's actions." Similarly, he said, people should not complain against laws limiting verbal abuse of the president and Congress.

The Federalists said it was a time of national emergency, and people had to support the government. They said the United States must present a united front to the French. As one Federalist newspaper put it: "He that is not for us, is against us."

The Republicans had been unable to prevent the passage of the Alien and Sedition Acts. Vice-President Jefferson decided to try an unusual way of opposing them. Secretly, he wrote that the Acts were unconstitutional. Then, he said that because each state had to vote for or against the Constitution, each state could decide if an act of Congress were unconstitutional. If a state decided a law was against the Constitution, then that law should not apply in that state.

Friends of Jefferson presented his writings to the Kentucky government. The state government voted its approval of the writings and thousands of copies were sent to other states. This became known as the Kentucky Resolution. James Madison had also secretly written similar ideas, and they were passed by the Virginia state government. No other states voted to support the Kentucky and Virginia Resolutions. It was not until many years later that people discovered who the true authors of the Resolutions were. Apparently they wrote them in secret to avoid being charged with sedition or even treason.

President Adams did not use the powers granted him by the Alien Acts. Many foreigners, however, for fear the president would exercise his powers, left the country. The Sedition Act was actively enforced and, as the Republicans had predicted, virtually all of those charged were Republicans. The first victim of the Sedition Act was a congressman from Vermont, Matthew Lyon.

In Congress, Lyon was an active opponent of the Federalist defense measures and controversial for other reasons. He was once almost expelled for fighting. Connecticut Congressman Griswold insulted Lyon and Lyon spit in his face. Later, the two men began clubbing one another while Congress was in session. For this incident Lyon was often called a beast—the spitting Lyon.

While back in Vermont, Lyon wrote an article claiming that Adams was interested in acting like a king. Although he knew he would be charged with breaking the law, Lyon continued writing. In another article he claimed the government was trying to make slaves of the people and seeking ties with the British monarchy. Lyon was charged, convicted, and thrown in jail. He could not believe that a congressman could be treated so badly. Neither could the voters in his district. While still in jail, Lyon was elected to another term in the Congress.

Another victim of the law was John Daly Burk. Burk had escaped from arrest in Ireland. He had started a riot by trying to rescue a man being led to his execution. Burk disguised himself as a woman and boarded a ship to the United States. He became a writer and eventually the editor of the *Time Piece*, a Republican newspaper in New York.

Burk hated the British monarch and wrote that Adams wanted to be king. He also accused Adams of falsifying diplomatic reports to make it appear that France wanted war. He said that Adams was favoring war with France. It was also reported that Burk said he wished the French would invade the United States and cut off the heads of all those supporting the Adams government.

Burk was arrested. Because he was not a citizen, the government said they would not press charges if he agreed to leave the United States. Burk agreed and said he would sail to Europe. Instead, however, he secretly went to Virginia. Jefferson and others had said that Virginia would be a safe place for people charged under the

Sedition Act. In Virginia, Burk changed his name and was not discovered by the authorities.

Not all those charged were writers. Late in 1798, President Adams was traveling through Newark, New Jersey. To honor him, flags were flown and cannons fired. One local resident, Luther Baldwin, became intoxicated and said that he wished the cannon would be fired at Adams' rear end. The tavern owner reported Baldwin. He was convicted of violating the Sedition Act and had to pay a stiff fine.

The battles with France came to an end. Changes in the French government's policy convinced Adams that they wanted peace. In October 1800, a peace agreement was signed.

The Federalist party also came to an end. Partly because of the increasing unpopularity of the Alien and Sedition Acts, the Federalists were never again a significant national power.

The Alien and Sedition Acts came to an end as well. They were legally in force for only a few years and expired when Jefferson became president.

The major sources for this story were:

Brodie, Fawn M. *Thomas Jefferson: An Intimate History.* New York: W. W. Norton, 1974.
Miller, John C. *Crisis in Freedom: The Alien and Sedition Acts.* Boston: Little, Brown, 1951.
Smith, James M. *Freedom's Fetters: The Alien and Sedition Laws and American Civil Liberties.*
  Ithaca, N.Y.: Cornell University Press, 1956.

ACTIVITIES FOR "THE PRICE OF FREE SPEECH"

Answer all questions on a separate sheet of paper.

Historical Understanding

Answer briefly:

1. What were two reasons that many Americans began to fear the French during the 1790s?

2. Political parties emerged during this time. What major differences existed between the Federalists and Republicans?

3. Why did the French begin attacking U.S. shipping?

Reviewing the Facts of the Case

Answer briefly:

1. What were the provisions of the Alien Acts?

2. What did the Sedition Act prohibit?

3. Why did Federalists support the Alien and Sedition laws? Why did Republicans oppose the Alien and Sedition laws?

4. What were the arguments set out in the Kentucky and Virginia Resolutions?

5. Lyon, Burk, and Baldwin all got in trouble with the law. What did each person do in violation of the law?

Analyzing Ethical Issues

The following are some values involved in this story:

LIBERTY: A value concerning what freedoms people should have and the limits that may be justifiably placed upon them.

EQUALITY: A value concerning whether people should be treated in the same way.

AUTHORITY: A value concerning what people or rules should be obeyed and the consequences for disobedience.

TRUTH: A value concerning the expression, distortion, or withholding of accurate information.

PROMISE-KEEPING: A value concerning the nature of duties that arise when promises are made.

Choose three of the values and describe an incident in which each was involved, as illustrated in this example:

VALUE	INCIDENT
Promise-keeping	*Washington's decision to proclaim neutrality in the war between England and France despite the treaty agreement of 1778 in which the United States said it would help France in case of war.*

Expressing Your Reasoning

1. Supporters of the Sedition Act made many arguments favoring it. Choose one of the arguments below that you think is a strong argument and write, in a few sentences, why you think it is a strong argument. Then, choose one of the arguments that you think is a weak one and state, in a few sentences, why you think it is a weak argument.
   a. In a time of national emergency, normal freedoms have to be limited.
   b. Constitutional guarantees of free expression do not mean people can say anything they feel like.
   c. A government has the right to protect itself from those who oppose it from within or without the country.
   d. People should be loyal and support their government and its leaders.
   e. Congress passed the law after fair debate and it should be obeyed during the few years it was to be in effect. New leaders could be voted in at the next election if people didn't like the law.

2. Opponents of the Sedition Act made many arguments against it. Choose one of the arguments below that you think is a strong argument and write, in a few sentences, why you think it is a strong argument. Then, choose one of the arguments that you think is a weak one and state, in a few sentences, why you think it is a weak argument.
   a. The First Amendment says that government should not interfere with the freedoms of speech and press.
   b. No formal war existed with France, so such severe limits on freedom were not necessary.
   c. The law was going to be used by the Federalists to attack Republican speakers and writers.
   d. Governmental leaders are selected by the people, and the people have a right to say whatever they wish about them.
   e. The law gave too much power to the president and the central government.
   f. In a democracy, people have a right to hear all sides on a question, so all opinions should be allowed.

3. A tavern owner reported Luther Baldwin's remarks to the authorities. He believed that a good citizen would do that. Was he right or

wrong in what he did? Should citizens always report violations of the law? Write a paragraph explaining your reasoning on these questions. Does it make a difference if the citizen opposes the law that he or she sees being violated?

4. *Seeking Additional Information.* In making decisions about such questions as those above, we often feel we need more information before we are satisfied with our judgments. Choose one of the above questions about which you would want more information than is presented in the story. What additional information would you like? Why would that information help you make a more satisfactory decision?

Denmark's Gamble
in South Carolina

DENMARK VESEY

Slave Quarters on South Carolina Plantation

Slavery existed in America from the earliest days of colonization. There were slaves in Jamestown, the first permanent English colony in North America. The existence of slavery has had a powerful effect on the course of American history.

Slavery was practiced throughout the colonies. There were slaves in New England as well as in the Southern Colonies. Many New England shipowners made money through the slave trade.

Although the practice of slavery was widespread, not all Americans felt it was right. When writing the Declaration of Independence, Thomas Jefferson, himself a slaveowner, wanted to include a statement saying that slavery was wrong. Representatives from South Carolina and Georgia opposed the statement. For the sake of colonial unity, the antislavery statement was not included in the final copy.

The Declaration said that "all men are created equal" but such a concept did not apply to slaves. Even though slaves were human beings, they were treated like private property. Like work animals, they could be bought or sold.

As years went by, slavery became concentrated in the South. Northern states gradually made slavery illegal. In the Southern states, however, slavery was believed necessary for the economy and it was not made illegal. Plantation owners believed that they could not make a profit without the use of slave labor.

In 1793, Eli Whitney invented the cotton gin. This machine made it easier to prepare cotton for market. As a result, much more cotton could be grown for sale. In 1791, South Carolina produced 15 million pounds of cotton. By 1812, production had risen to 50 million pounds. As South Carolina and other states became more dependent on a cotton economy, they also became more dependent on slaves. More and more slaves were used to work on the plantations.

There were South Carolinians who opposed slavery. Some economists argued that slavery was not good for the economy. They said the cost of housing, feeding, and caring for slaves cut back the profits that cotton growers could make. They thought it would be cheaper to hire workers rather than keep slaves. Other opponents of slavery, like Angelina and Sarah Grimke, argued that slavery was morally wrong. Arguments against slavery were not effective at making it illegal in the South.

Slaves sometimes attempted to revolt to gain their freedom. Whites often feared the possibility of slave revolts, and laws were passed to prevent their occurrence.

In South Carolina there were a number of laws governing how

slaves were to be treated. For example, it was against the law to teach slaves to write. This was intended to prevent slaves from organizing a large-scale rebellion through the sending of messages. It was illegal for more than seven slaves to travel on certain roads unless a white person was with them. Slaves who were away from their owners had to have written passes saying where they were going and for what purpose. Slaves without passes could be beaten if they were caught by the authorities. Slaves who committed crimes, like stealing, could be severely punished or executed. Whites who killed slaves would usually be fined, but slaves who killed whites, even in self-defense, were usually executed.

Not all blacks were slaves. Some were free, but there were special laws governing them. For example, free blacks could own property, but they could not vote. In trials, free blacks could not testify against whites, but slaves could testify against free blacks. Whites could testify against any black person. Blacks accused of crimes were not allowed trial by jury. A group of judges decided their cases. Free blacks had certain liberties, but they were not treated the same as whites.

As South Carolina became more dependent on cotton, it seemed unlikely that slavery would be abolished or the laws changed. One man, Denmark Vesey, eventually decided to take drastic action.

As a boy, Denmark was a slave on the island of St. Thomas in the West Indies. One day in 1781, a slavetrader, Captain Joseph Vesey, came to the island and loaded hundreds of slaves on his ship. Twelve-year-old Denmark was one of them. The captain and the crew were impressed with Denmark's intelligence and personality.

Captain Vesey took his slave cargo to St. Dominique, a rich French colony. Denmark and the other slaves were sold on the island. A few months later Captain Vesey returned and was told that young Denmark was an unfit slave because he seemed to have fits of epilepsy. As a result, the captain had to take Denmark back. He became the captain's personal slave, and by custom took the last name Vesey.

With Captain Vesey, Denmark sailed for many years. In the course of his travels he learned to speak French, Spanish, and Danish. He also learned firsthand of the horrors of the slave trade. He sailed to Africa where rum and other goods were traded for slaves. The slaves were brought to the West Indies or Southern states where those who survived the grim voyage were sold.

In 1783, Captain Vesey decided to settle in Charleston, South

Carolina, and become a merchant. The seafaring Denmark, now 16 years old, became a slave on land. Charleston was one of the largest cities in the United States and the major trading center in the South. In the Charleston area there were many more blacks than whites. According to the census of 1800, there were 63,615 blacks and 18,768 whites in the area. Most of the blacks were slaves.

City slaves had many different jobs. Some worked in the markets; some worked in the fishing business; still others were carpenters, butchers, blacksmiths, and painters. Owners often hired out their slaves to perform skilled labor for others.

By chance, Denmark Vesey became a free man. In 1800 he won $1,500 in a lottery, a form of gambling. He used $600 to buy his freedom from Captain Vesey. At the age of 33, Denmark Vesey was no longer a slave.

Vesey was a skilled carpenter and became known as one of the best workers in the area. He had a house and was able to save a substantial amount of money. He married several times. His wives were slaves, however, and he could only see them, or his children, with the permission of their owners. Although he was free, the effects of slavery were still with him.

Vesey hated slavery. With anyone who would talk with him, he argued that slavery was wrong. In later years, one slave, William Paul, said of Vesey: "He studied the Bible a great deal, and tried to prove from it that slavery and bondage is against the Bible." Vesey came to despise whites. According to Paul, "He said he would not like to have a white man in his presence—that he had a great hatred for the whites." Vesey urged blacks to walk with pride and dignity among the whites.

Vesey knew he was not alone in opposing slavery. He heard of the slave revolt on St. Dominique, where he had spent time as a slave. In 1791, the slaves staged a mass revolt. At least one thousand sugar and cocoa plantations were set aflame and hundreds of whites were killed. Some of the white survivors made their way to Charleston. Their stories heightened white fears of slave uprisings.

Vesey also heard of attempts by Northern abolitionists to get rid of slavery. He read articles and pamphlets opposing slavery. He also heard of debates about Missouri. In 1819, Missouri was about to become a state and there was heated argument about whether it should be a free or slave state. Vesey was impressed with the anti-slavery arguments in the debate.

Vesey also knew there had been attempted slave revolts in the

United States. In 1800, for example, a Virginia slave, Gabriel Prosser, organized an army of slaves and attempted to attack Richmond. Two slaves informed the authorities of the coming attack, and Governor James Monroe gathered troops and put an end to Prosser's plan. Over thirty slaves were hanged for trying to rebel.

Although it was dangerous, Denmark Vesey became determined to lead a slave rebellion. To succeed, he knew it had to be carefully planned, well organized, and kept secret. He had been lucky in the lottery, but it would take more than luck to win this time.

Late in 1821 he called together a small group of men he thought he could trust. They would help him lead the revolt. Ned and Rolla Bennett, servants of the governor, Thomas Bennett, agreed to join. Peter Poyas, a skilled ship carpenter and strong leader, agreed. Gullah Jack, a slave whom some thought had mystical powers, joined. At least two other slaves, Monday Gell and Jack Purcell, also joined the original group of leaders.

In secret meetings more were recruited to the plan. Vesey and others were careful that their plot would not be discovered by anyone. Peter Poyas warned, "Take care and don't mention it to those waiting men who received presents of old coats from their masters or they'll betray us."

The plan was complex. Slaves in the surrounding countryside were recruited. Gullah Jack told some of them that his magic would protect them. Weapons were obtained and stored in secret places. Points of attack were planned carefully to assure success. Some have estimated that nine thousand were eventually organized for the revolt. Many slaves refused to join. They were told they would be killed if they revealed the plot. One slave reported that Vesey opened a meeting saying "he had an important secret to communicate to us, which we must not disclose to anyone, and if we did, we should be put to instant death."

The date for the revolt was to be Sunday, July 14, 1822. On Sunday blacks from the countryside commonly visited in the city. The action was to begin at midnight. One group, led by Rolla Bennett, would kill Governor Bennett and the mayor. Other groups would attack arsenals and other places where guns and ammunition were stored. Still other groups would ride through the streets killing any who might sound a warning. After capturing weapons, the rebels would kill all whites in the area and any blacks who refused to join in. Quoting selected passages from the Bible, Vesey ordered that women and children should also be killed.

The plan was set but it was not to succeed. In spite of Poyas' warning, William Paul tried to recruit a "house slave," Peter Prioleau. Paul talked to him in May, but Prioleau refused to join. After thinking it over Prioleau decided to tell his owners that a slave revolt was being planned.

The governor and mayor were told of the planned revolt but they did not know the details. William Paul was arrested, held in jail, intently questioned, and possibly tortured. He eventually identified two leaders of the plot. They were arrested but acted so innocently that they were released.

In the meantime, Major John Wilson, having heard rumors of the revolt, began a private investigation. He asked a trusted slave, George Wilson, to do some spying. On June 14, George brought back shocking news. There was to be a revolt and it was going to begin in two days! Having heard of the arrests, Vesey decided to act a month earlier than planned.

The authorities moved quickly. Troops were placed on guard. They protected the areas where weapons were stored. Vesey learned that officials had been warned and, as the hour for the revolt approached, he decided it was too risky. The revolt was called off.

An investigation was organized and suspected slaves were arrested. The arrested slaves were questioned and, according to some witnesses, tortured. Peter Poyas said, "Do not open your lips! Die silent, as you shall see me do." Most followed his command but some broke under the pressure and began revealing names and details. Soon Denmark Vesey and others were arrested.

In all, 131 blacks were arrested. Of these 53 were found innocent; 43 were banished from the state; and 35 were hanged. Among those sentenced to death were Peter Poyas, Ned and Rolla Bennett, Gullah Jack, and Denmark Vesey.

When pronouncing the sentence, the judge said to the 55-year-old Vesey:

> Your professed design was to trample all laws . . . to riot in blood . . . to introduce anarchy and confusion in their most horrid forms. Your life has become, therefore, a just and necessary sacrifice. . . . You were a free man; were comparatively wealthy; and enjoyed every comfort compatible with your situation. You had, therefore, much to risk and little to gain. From your age and experience, you ought to have known that success was impracticable.

A moment's reflection must have convinced you, that the ruin of your race would have been the probable result, and that years would have rolled away before they could have recovered that confidence which they once enjoyed in this community.

One result of the attempted revolt was the passage of harsh new laws. One was called the Negro Seamen's Act. According to this law, any free blacks working on ships entering Charleston Harbor were to be put in jail until the ship left.

The federal government opposed this law, and it was declared unconstitutional because it violated the central government's right to make treaties. A treaty with England permitted ships' crews to move about freely when in U.S. ports. South Carolina said the federal government had no right to interfere with its right to make laws protecting itself. Debate over the Negro Seamen's Act was one instance of a growing disagreement about the rights of the states and the rights of the federal government. This general disagreement over states' rights was a major factor that led to the Civil War.

The major sources for this story were:

The Trial Record of Denmark Vesey, with an introduction by John O. Killens. Boston: Beacon Press, 1970.

Lofton, John. *Insurrection in South Carolina: The Turbulent World of Denmark Vesey*. Yellow Springs, Ohio: The Antioch Press, 1964.

ACTIVITIES FOR "DENMARK'S GAMBLE IN SOUTH CAROLINA"

Answer all questions on a separate piece of paper.

Historical Understanding

Answer briefly:

1. How did the invention of the cotton gin affect the Southern economy?

2. Describe three of the laws that restricted slaves.

3. The Grimke sisters and some economists opposed slavery. What was the major difference between their arguments against slavery?

4. Why wasn't an antislavery statement included in the Declaration of Independence?

5. How did Vesey's slave revolt bring South Carolina into conflict with the federal government?

Reviewing the Facts of the Case

Answer briefly:

1. How did Denmark Vesey become a free man?

2. Many things led to Vesey's antislavery beliefs. What were three sources of his antislavery arguments?

3. How did the authorities discover the planned revolt?

4. Why did Vesey call off the slave rebellion?

Analyzing Ethical Issues

An ethical question asks whether something is right or wrong, fair or unfair. Such questions involve values.
For example:

QUESTION	VALUE INVOLVED
Was it fair for the law to treat blacks differently from whites?	*Equality*

Choose three of the values defined below. Then look back over the story and write an ethical question for each of the three values, as illustrated in the example above. Indicate which of the values is involved in each of your questions.

AUTHORITY: A value concerning what rules or people should be obeyed and the consequences for disobedience.

LIBERTY: A value concerning what freedoms people should have and the limits that may be justifiably placed upon them.

LIFE: A value concerning when, if ever, it is justifiable to threaten or take the life of another.

PROMISE-KEEPING: A value concerning the nature of duties which arise when promises are made.

PROPERTY: A value concerning what people should be allowed to own and how they should be allowed to use it.

TRUTH: A value concerning the expression, distortion, or withholding of accurate information.

Expressing Your Reasoning

1. At the trial the judge gave Vesey a lecture in which he told Vesey why he should not have tried to organize a rebellion. Reread the judge's statement. Do you agree with what he said? Why or why not?

2. Was it right to punish Denmark Vesey even though the revolt was cancelled and no one was hurt? Write a paragraph explaining your answer to the question.

3. William Paul tried to get Peter Prioleau to join the revolt. Prioleau refused to join and told his owners of the planned revolt. Should he have told? Why or why not?

4. *Seeking Additional Information.* In making decisions about such questions as those above we often feel we need more information before we are satisfied with our judgments. Choose one of the above questions about which you would want more information than is presented in the story. What additional information would you like? Why would that information help you make a more satisfactory decision?

A Woman's Place
Is in the Factory

LOWELL MILL STRIKES

Power Loom Weaving in Textile Mill, 1835

In the early 1800s, many changes occurred in the United States. The building of roads, canals, and railroads allowed for faster and better transportation. Thousands of settlers moved west to farm newly available land. Large numbers of immigrants entered the country. The population was growing. In 1850 there were 23 million people in the United States, more than twice as many as in 1820. One of the most important changes, especially in the North, was the growth of manufacturing.

The textile industry was one of the first large-scale manufacturing systems. The invention of machines for making thread and weaving cloth made it profitable for business people to build factories in which cloth could be made. The machines required waterpower to run them. New England had ample supplies of waterpower, and that region soon became the leader in textile manufacturing.

The machines needed waterpower, but they also needed people-power. People were needed to work the machines. The factory owners knew they needed a skilled and dependable work force if the textile mills were to be successful. Some factory owners hired men, children, and sometimes entire families. Francis Cabot Lowell, one of the owners of the Boston Manufacturing Company in Waltham, Massachusetts, devised a different system. He found the best work force to be girls and young women. His system became world famous.

Lowell died in 1816, but his ideas remained alive. His successors at the Boston Manufacturing Company decided to build more factories. They bought land near the rapids of the Merrimack River and set about building factories and boardinghouses for the women workers.

The designers tried to make the area as beautiful as possible. The brick or wood boardinghouses were sturdy and more attractive than the houses of workers elsewhere. Trees and shrubs were planted and the factories laid out so that pleasant views of the river and countryside could be seen. Experts were hired to build the factories, waterwheels, and machinery. By 1824 the mills had begun production.

In 1826 the growing town was named Lowell. It became dependent on the developing textile industry. An editorial in a local newspaper said: "The growth and prosperity of this town depends altogether upon the success of the manufacturing establishments, which have literally made it what it now is. . . . To oppose the manufacturing interests would be nothing less than suicidal."

The area did become prosperous. The companies built a school, library facilities, a fire company, and a church. Business was good and the town an appealing place. A visitor reported:

> Several school-houses were pointed out to me, and no less than three churches; besides innumerable boarding houses, taverns, newspaper offices, watch-makers, bookshops, hatters, comb-makers, and all the family of stores, every one of them as fresh and new as if the bricks had been in the mold by yesterday.

What made Lowell world famous was its working force of young, skilled, and intelligent women. By 1833 about 3,800 of the 5,000 mill workers were girls and young women.

In those times women had few legal rights. Women could not vote. Husbands did not have to include their wives in their wills. Money earned by a woman could be taken by her husband to pay his debts. In many ways women were considered unproductive and a burden on society.

As a general rule a woman's place was in the home. She cooked, sewed, and handled various family matters. Above all else a woman had to show she was religious and proper in the way she led her life. A woman who got a bad reputation was scorned by the people who knew her.

There were times when the rural women of New England had to try to make money to help support their families and themselves. Few jobs were open to women, and the pay was not high. Women who worked as household help might earn 50 cents to a dollar a week. Women who went from house to house offering their services as weavers or seamstresses might receive 75 cents a week. When women were hired as teachers, their pay was even less than that of servants and seamstresses.

Money was scarce for the farming families. Farmers often traded their products to obtain necessary supplies. Farmers did need money, however, to help pay their debts and, when possible, to send their sons to college. The cash paid to factory workers was a great attraction.

Factory workers were paid six to seven times as much as teachers. Beginners might earn 55 cents a week while more skilled workers could earn four dollars or more. The average earnings were about two dollars a week.

Money was not the only thing that attracted workers to Lowell.

Rural life was often drab, lonely, and boring. In Lowell there was the excitement of meeting new people. There were shops where clothing and other goods could be bought. There were also opportunities to become better educated and to develop a feeling of usefulness and independence.

The factory owners knew that they could not attract women workers unless it was clear their reputations would remain pure. Families would not let their women work in a degrading or disreputable atmosphere. The companies stressed the uplifting life in the boardinghouses. They made it clear that the women would be required to attend church services and that those that operated the boardinghouses were upstanding religious women.

When a woman was hired she signed an agreement with the company. This contract stated that she would work for 12 months, give two weeks notice if she was going to quit, live in the boardinghouses, observe all the rules, not be absent from work unless ill, be home by ten o'clock each night, and not engage in improper conduct.

The older women who ran the boardinghouses also worked for the companies. They paid a small amount of rent to the companies and received a set amount of money for each worker who lived there. This money was used to buy food and other necessities for running the houses. The money was deducted directly from each worker's wages.

Those who ran the boardinghouses agreed to supervise the women and to make sure they obeyed the ten o'clock curfew and other regulations. In addition, the housekeepers had to see that no undesirable visitors came to the houses and make sure the women behaved properly.

The benefits of working in Lowell did not come easily, however. The work day was typically 12 to 13 hours long. The workers' time was regulated by a loud bell. Work usually was from five in the morning until the final bell at seven in the evening. One-half hour was allowed for each meal. This was the pattern of work for six days a week.

Famous people visited Lowell and were impressed. President Andrew Jackson remarked about the workers' beauty and grace. Davy Crockett praised the workers and the factory owners. Author Charles Dickens was impressed with the *Lowell Offering*, a magazine written by some of the women. In it they published articles, poems, and stories. The fact that workers could find time to publish a high-quality magazine helped make the Lowell system known throughout the world.

As time went by many workers began to think the Lowell system was not such a great achievement. By 1836 those who ran the boardinghouses were finding it difficult to provide proper meals and service. Prices for goods had gone up. The owners of the factories decided to deduct an extra twelve-and-one-half cents from each worker's weekly pay. This money went directly to the housekeepers.

Many workers were angered by this new deduction from their pay. It amounted to a wage cut of about 5 percent. They began to talk of going on strike; refusing to work until their pay was returned. Harriet Hanson, an 11-year-old worker, favored a strike. One day in 1836 she and about fifteen hundred workers "turned out." They walked out of the factories.

The turn out lasted for only a few days and was unsuccessful. The owners did not change their wage-cut policy and the workers returned to their jobs. The owners were determined to show they would not tolerate strikes. Harriet Hanson's widowed mother operated a boarding-house. Because her daughter was one of the strikers, an agent of the company fired Mrs. Hanson. He told her: "Mrs. Hanson, you could not prevent the older girls from turning out, but your daughter is a child, and *her* you could control."

The owners had another way of dealing with disruptive workers—the *blacklist*. Factory managers would put the names of any workers who they thought were troublemakers on a list. The list was shared with the managers of other factories. A person whose name was on the blacklist would then be unable to get a job in another factory after being fired from one. One list in 1829 included the names of women charged with "mutiny," "disobedience to orders," and "dissatisfaction with wages."

Workers despised the blacklist, but they soon had more to upset them. In the late 1830s and early 1840s, the factory owners' profits began to decline. There were two major reasons for this. The price of cotton, the main raw material, had increased. Also, many new factories had been built, and the amount of cloth being made increased. As the supply of cloth went up, its selling price came down. In the 1820s, the owners' profits were about nine cents on each yard of cloth. By 1850 they were sometimes making only one-half cent a yard. Although the profits were declining, the companies still were making money.

The owners thought there were two ways of fighting falling profits. One was to cut the workers' wages, thus reducing the cost of production. The other was to get each worker to produce more, thus in-

creasing the amount of cloth that could be sold. Both methods were
used. Wages were occasionally cut and rarely raised. To increase
production, each weaver was required to work more looms. In some
cases the workers had to work four looms instead of the usual one or
two.

As a result of these policies many workers became dissatisfied with
their working conditions. In 1844, Sarah Bagley and some other
women organized the Female Labor Reform Association. Sarah
Bagley accused the companies of making too much money and not
caring about the workers. She and others urged the state to pass a law
reducing the work day to ten hours instead of twelve.

As a general rule, the association opposed strikes unless all other
methods of change failed. One of the methods was to hold conventions. These conventions passed resolutions and sent petitions to the
state legislature. Women who attended the conventions were urged to
tell their employers that they were not at work because of illness. For
unexcused absences the women would probably have been blacklisted.

Sarah Bagley also wrote for the *Voice of Industry*, a labor publication dedicated to improving the workers' condition. In 1846, when
one of the companies tried to get its workers to tend four looms
instead of three, a group of women pledged they would not do it
unless their wages were increased. Any woman who refused to take
the pledge was to have her name printed in the *Voice of Industry*, as a
"traitor" to the reform movement. Virtually all the workers signed the
pledge, and the company did not institute its intended policy.

Attempts to get a ten-hour work day were not successful. The
Lowell representative to the state legislature, William Schouler, led a
committee that agreed to investigate working conditions. The committee listened to Bagley and others who spoke of long hours, hot
work rooms, failing health of some workers, and other problems. The
committee visited Lowell factories and finally concluded the ten-hour
day was not needed. In its report, the committee said: "Labor is
intelligent enough to make its own bargains, and look out for its own
interests without any interference from us."

The committee's attitude was shared by many legislators. A Senate
committee concluded that the legislature should not get involved. It
said the state should not "deprive the citizen of his freedom of
contract." The claim was that workers freely agreed to work in the
factories. As one writer put it, "It is a most perfect democracy. Any of
its subjects can depart from it at pleasure without the least restraint."

Bagley and others were disgusted with the Schouler committee decision. Even though women did not have the right to vote, they worked hard to prevent him from being re-elected. Schouler was defeated in the next election.

Schouler was angered by Bagley's efforts to defeat him. He tried to find something that would damage her reputation. He could find nothing scandalous about her, but one of her associates, John Cluer, was not so lucky. Schouler printed charges that Cluer was an immoral drunkard and a gossip who opposed organized religion. Schouler's charges helped cast doubt on Sarah Bagley and her movement. She gradually ended her active involvement in reform and reportedly suffered a breakdown.

Lowell's reputation as an ideal factory system soon faded. To keep wages low, more and more poor Irish immigrants were hired to replace the native-born New England women. By 1850 about 50 percent of the workers were recently arrived Irish. Reformers continued to work for improvements, but it was not until 1874 that the ten-hour work day became required by law.

The major sources for this story were:

Josephson, Hannah. *The Golden Threads*. New York: Duell, Sloan and Pearce, 1949.

Robinson, Harriet. *Loom and Spindle*, with an introduction by Jane W. Pultz. Kailua, Hawaii: Press Pacifica, 1976.

Ware, Caroline F. *The Early New England Cotton Manufacture*. New York: Russell and Russell, 1966.

ACTIVITIES FOR "A WOMAN'S PLACE IS IN THE FACTORY"

Answer all questions on a separate sheet of paper.

Historical Understanding

Answer briefly:

1. Identify two important changes that occurred in American society during the early 1800s.

2. What were two reasons that textile manufacturing developed in New England?

3. Describe three ways that women were treated differently from men during the early 1800s.

Reviewing the Facts of the Case

Answer briefly:

1. Why were young women attracted to the Lowell factories?

2. Why did the Lowell system become world famous?

3. Why was Harriet Hanson's mother fired?

4. What was the *blacklist*?

5. Why did manufacturers' profits fall during the 1830s and 1840s?

6. How did the manufacturers try to keep up their profits?

7. What was the purpose of the Female Labor Reform Association?

8. What reason did the state legislators give for refusing to pass the ten-hour law?

Analyzing Ethical Issues

There are a number of times in this story when people made ethical decisions. Ethical decisions involve judgments that affect the rights or well-being of others. For example:

> *The employers' use of the blacklist was an ethical decision affecting the rights of the workers.*

List three other instances from the story in which people made ethical decisions.

Expressing Your Reasoning

1. Women attending reform conventions were urged to tell their employers that they were ill on the days they were absent. In this way they could be kept off the blacklist. Would a worker be right to do this? Why or why not?

2. The *Voice of Industry* would list as "traitors" any women who refused to sign a pledge against working on more looms. Would it be right to do this? Why or why not?

3. The legislature refused to pass the ten-hour day law because they did not want to interfere with citizens' freedom of contract. Do you agree or disagree with that decision? Explain your reasoning.

4. Sarah Bagley and others felt the companies were making too much money and not improving the working conditions in the factories. There were no laws limiting the profits that companies could make. Abbot Lawrence, one of the company leaders, once said: "If you are troubled with the belief that I am growing too rich, there is one thing that you may as well understand: I know how to make money, and you cannot prevent it." Should any restrictions have been placed on the companys' profits? Why or why not? Write a paragraph explaining your point of view.

5. Choose one of the instances you have identified in which people made an ethical decision. Do you think the decision was right or wrong? Explain why you thought it was right or wrong.

6. *Seeking Additional Information.* In making decisions about such questions as those above, we often feel we need more information before we are satisfied with our judgments. Choose one of the above questions about which you would want more information than is presented in the story. What additional information would you like? How would that information help you make a more satisfactory decision?

An Unconquered Indian

OSCEOLA

Osceola (from George Catlin original portrait)

Soon after gaining their independence from England many Americans moved westward beyond the narrow coastal plain of the Atlantic. These pioneers braved the wilderness in search of land for farms and plantations. In the Southeast, white settlers steadily encroached on the lands of the Creek Indians.

It was in 1813 that war broke out between the Creeks of Georgia and the United States. The war ended the following year after General Jackson attacked a large Creek force, killing a thousand warriors. Fighting during the war forced migration of the Creeks from Georgia into Florida. There they joined Seminoles who had migrated to Florida during the previous century. Among the migrating Creeks was a boy, later called Osceola, who was to become one of the most famous figures in Florida history.

Osceola was born in 1804 in Georgia. His mother was a Creek Indian and his father a white trader. Like other Creeks of mixed blood with a Creek mother, Osceola considered himself an Indian. He learned to kill squirrels with a bow and arrow and joined other boys for moonlight hunts after opossums and racoons. He developed stealth in the woods that served him well in the future as a warrior.

The Creek War came close to young Osceola. He and his mother fled with other refugees from one hiding place to another. By the war's end they had drifted to Florida and settled among the Seminoles. Osceola grew into manhood as a Seminole living north of present-day Tampa.

Soon after the Creek War ended, the First Seminole War began. A major cause of the war was conflict over black slaves. Many had escaped from plantations to take refuge among the Seminoles in Florida. Southern slaveholders were furious and insisted that the army capture runaway slaves and return them to their owners.

Major General Andrew Jackson was dispatched to the scene in March 1818. His troops fought several engagements with the Seminoles in Spanish-owned Florida. The Seminoles were finally driven south to the area around Tampa Bay. Jackson withdrew, ending the war.

After the First Seminole War it became clear to the Spanish that they had little control over Florida. It was turned over to the United States in 1819. Article 6 of the treaty with Spain stated that the inhabitants of Florida were to be "admitted to the enjoyment of all privileges, rights, and immunities of the citizens of the United States."

United States policy toward the Seminoles was to keep them, at least temporarily, in Florida. Pressure increased on the government to move the Indians westward. White southerners claimed that unless the Indians were driven out of Florida, slaves would continue to join them. This pressure led in 1823 to the Treaty of Moultrie Creek. Under the threat of renewed warfare, the leading chiefs, representing a majority of the Seminoles, signed the treaty. It had four major provisions.

1. The Seminoles gave up claim to the whole territory of Florida except for a 4-million-acre reservation.
2. The U.S. government provided a cash payment of $5,000 a year for 20 years, plus livestock and farm implements.
3. The Indians were to prevent runaway slaves from entering the reservation.
4. Whites would not be permitted to hunt, settle, or intrude on the reservation.

The reservation boundaries were cut off from the Florida coasts, so fishing was no longer possible for the Indians. Furthermore, the reservation land was poor for agriculture. A few inches of topsoil covered a base of white sand. If plowed for any length of time the sand became dominant. About a year after the Treaty of Moultrie Creek was signed most Seminoles experienced severe hunger. Some died of starvation.

By this time Osceola had risen to the position of Seminole war chief. He was an outstanding athlete, deeply admired for his physical skills by other Indians. Despite harsh conditions on the Seminole reservation, Osceola was determined to enforce the terms of the Moultrie Creek Treaty. He did not want his people to be forced to move westward. Conditions west of the Mississippi, where traditional enemies of the Seminoles lived, would be even worse for his people. With a small band of followers, he began police actions to prevent young Seminoles from harming whites or stealing white people's property. This he believed necessary if the Seminoles were to avoid being forced out of Florida. Many Seminoles, nearly starving, raided white men's cattle. Several murders were also committed. Osceola helped bring some of the offenders to justice.

Conflict over land, slaves, and cattle persisted between the Seminoles and the whites. The hatchet descended when Andrew Jackson became president. In May 1830, the Removal Act was passed by Congress and signed by the president. The new law provided that the government could trade land in the West for Indian land in the East.

Under the law the government could do whatever was necessary to remove the Indians to the new land. The Removal Act was designed to expand white settlement by moving the Indians out of the southeastern states.

In accordance with the Removal Act, a conference was called in 1832 between white officials and Seminole chiefs. They met at a place called Payne's Landing, near Fort King, the army post near the Seminole reservation. At the conference a treaty was signed. The Treaty of Payne's Landing provided that a party of Seminole chiefs would be sent to examine the country west of the Mississippi River. If the chiefs thought the country suitable, they would agree to move their people there to live. Several leading Seminole chiefs did not sign the Payne's Landing Treaty. It was, however, ratified by the U.S. Senate and proclaimed by President Jackson.

The following year a party of Seminole chiefs examined the proposed reservation beyond the Mississippi and found it to their liking. Upon returning, without consulting the other chiefs, they signed an agreement on behalf of their nation. The agreement stated that they were well satisfied with the location provided for them, and that they would begin removal to their new homeland as soon as the federal government made arrangements.

When they heard what the delegation of chiefs had agreed to, many Seminole leaders, including Osceola, were outraged. They insisted that the chiefs who agreed to removal had no authority to speak for all Seminoles. The prestige of Osceola increased as resistance to emigration grew. At a private council of Seminole chiefs, he said:

> If we must fight, we will fight. . . . I hope we don't have to fight the white man, but if it happens, every one of our warriors will be ready . . . the white people got some of our chiefs to sign a paper to give our lands to them; but our chiefs did not do as we told them to do. They did wrong; we must do right.

Osceola had now assumed leadership of the Seminole nation. The chiefs, except those favoring removal, were united behind him.

Because resistance to the Payne's Landing Treaty grew, the military commander of all troops in Florida called a meeting in 1835. The purpose of the meeting was to gain acceptance for peaceful removal. A large number of Seminole chiefs assembled for the meeting. Most were bitter and defiant. They protested the Payne's Landing Treaty, claiming it did not represent the desires of the Seminole nation.

After listening to the protests of several chiefs, the U.S. Indian Agent for the Florida Territory, General Wiley Thompson, addressed the chiefs. He picked up a document from the conference table and read it aloud, pausing for the translator. The document asserted that the Payne's Landing Treaty was valid.

Thompson insisted that the Seminoles had agreed to go West. He demanded that the chiefs confirm the Payne's Landing Treaty by signing the new document. Eight of the thirteen chiefs around the table signed. Five of the leading chiefs refused. Thompson, red with anger, picked up another paper. It was a list of Seminole chiefs. Seizing a pen, he made five slashes on the roll. He then faced the Indians and said, "I have removed five names from the roll of the chiefs. These men no longer represent the Seminole Nation." Thompson's actions made one point clear to the Indians: removal would be enforced with or without their consent.

Thompson's action of deposing the chiefs was a deadly insult. When his words had been translated, a roar of anger arose from the deposed chiefs. There were wild shrieks from warriors around the meeting tent. Finally, calm was restored by the eight chiefs who had signed.

General Thompson now wanted the subchiefs who were present to sign the document. Some of them came forward and made their marks on the paper. Osceola stood silently with his arms folded. Thompson read his name, signaling that he should step forward to sign. In his graceful catlike manner, he approached the table, gazing sternly into Thompson's eyes. With a sweeping motion he suddenly drew his hunting knife and stabbed savagely through the paper on the table. With this defiant gesture he cried out, "This is the only way I sign!" Amidst the shock of white officials, Osceola yanked out his knife and calmly walked away. The flash of his knife was a hint of what was to come.

Osceola, more than any other Seminole leader, inspired his people to fight rather than move West. He became a symbol of Indian resistance to white domination. That resistance led to the Second Seminole War, the costliest ever fought against the American Indian. It resulted in fifteen hundred deaths among white soldiers and cost the United States almost 40 million dollars, an enormous sum for the times.

In June 1835, before hostilities broke out, Osceola paid a final visit to Wiley Thompson in his office at Fort King. Osceola had come to complain about the general's recent ban on the sale of arms and powder to the Indians. Thompson was still angry about Osceloa's refusal to sign the document approving the Payne's Landing Treaty. An argument broke out. Osceola flew into a flurry and stormed out of the agent's office. Thompson ordered four soldiers to overtake him. As they dragged Osceola back to the fort he shouted, "I shall remember this hour! The agent has his day, I will have mine!"

Osceola was placed in irons and confined to the guardhouse. By nightfall his fury abated, and he was able to think clearly. Thompson, he thought, must be killed for this terrible insult. Meanwhile he needed a means of being released. He decided to lie. He apologized to Thompson, agreed to sign the paper confirming the Payne's Landing Treaty, and promised to urge other Seminoles to move West. The irons were struck and Osceola left the guardhouse in silence, revenge on his mind.

Matters moved toward disaster. A council of Seminole chiefs met and decided to resist removal forcibly. The chiefs appointed Osceola head war chief. They also decided that those chiefs who favored removal be treated like enemies and killed.

One chief who believed in emigration was Charley Emathla. Osceola led four hundred warriors to Charley Emathla's village where they surrounded the chief's lodge. They demanded that the chief pledge himself and his people to resist removal. The chief protested, saying that the only hope of being saved from total destruction was to go West. Osceola and 12 companions ambushed the chief the next day and shot him to death.

Hostilities between Seminoles and soldiers began in December 1835. During the early days of the war, Osceola's enemy, General Wiley Thompson, still believed the Indians could be coerced into removal. Midday on December 28, 1835, he walked from his office at Fort King to the officer's mess for lunch. After a leisurely meal Thompson took a stroll outside the fort. When he did not return, a party was sent out to search for him. His body was found stabbed, scalped, and riddled with fourteen bullets. Osceola had taken his revenge against the Indian agent.

Full-scale warfare was now in progress. Osceola's grasp of tactics was excellent. Hit-and-run attacks by the Seminoles were successful. The white soldiers were trained for open combat on battlefields. They were unprepared for repeated ambushes by Seminole warriors concealed in the swamps and forests of Florida. In addition to attacks on soldiers, Seminole bands plundered the civilian settlements along the east coast of the peninsula. Plantations were attacked and burned as far south as Miami.

Characteristic of combat early in the war was an incident now known as Dade's Massacre. On a cold December morning in 1835, 108 men under the command of Major Francis Dade were marching along the Little Withlacoochee River toward Fort King. The soldiers gnawed at cold field rations. They plowed through the mud, often waist-deep in swamp water. Mosquitoes and flies bit their necks. Alligators lay on the surface of adjacent sands. It was a struggle for the soldiers to keep their cartridge boxes and weapons dry. They were also frightened that Seminole warriors might be hiding in the woods, waiting to ambush them.

Suddenly the morning silence was shattered as a single shot rang out in the mist. Major Dade slumped in his saddle. An ear-splitting assault by Seminole warriors followed. The soldiers barely had a chance to return the fire. By the end of the assault 107 soldiers were killed and only 3 Seminoles.

Osceola was winning his war. U.S. generals had been unable to subdue the Seminoles. This gave Osceola little satisfaction, however. He knew that in the long run the superior forces of the whites could overcome his people. His goal was now to secure an honorable peace before the Seminole will to resist disintegrated.

As the war became a stalemate, Osceola decided to discuss a possible peace with General Thomas Jessup, commander of U.S. forces. Jessup had only one goal in mind: stop the war by stopping Osceola. Other Seminole leaders were important, but they were mere shadows when compared to Osceola. Recently Jessup had received a note from Osceola claiming he could hold out against the total forces of the United States for five years.

In October 1837, Osceola arrived near St. Augustine with about one hundred warriors to engage Jessup in peace talks. A white flag of truce flew above the Seminole camp. General Jessup sent an officer to talk with Osceola at his camp. While they spoke, soldiers encircled the Indian camp and closed it in. No shots were fired. The Seminoles were armed but it was too late to resist. Osceola was captured and placed in a cell at Fort Marion, an old Spanish prison.

Soon after his capture, Osceola had an opportunity to escape with his companions. The Indian prisoners were confined in a small dungeon of the prison lighted only by a small opening in the wall. There were two metal bars across the opening. On the night of October 21, 1837, one of the bars, which was either rusted or loose, was removed by one of the Indians. With one bar removed, the prisoners managed to squeeze with great difficulty through the opening. The sharp stones scraped skin off their bodies. Earlier they had cut up the bags given to them to sleep on. The shredded bags furnished the material for a rope which they used to reach the ground below. Twenty Seminoles escaped from their Fort Marion cell that night and made their way safely back to a Seminole encampment. Osceola refused to join his cellmates in their escape. When asked why he had not joined those who escaped, he proudly replied, "I have done nothing to be ashamed of; it is for those to feel shame who entrapped me."

On January 30, 1838, Osceola died of malaria in prison. Though a few chiefs continued to fight, Seminole resistance began to crumble. By 1842, the war had sputtered to an end. A small number of Seminoles retreated to the Everglades. Most were removed west to Oklahoma.

The major sources for this story were:

Coe, Charles. *Red Patriots* (facsimile reproduction of 1891 edition). Gainesville: The University of Florida Press, 1974.

Hartley, William, and Hartley, Ellen. *Osceola: The Unconquered Indian.* New York: Hawthorn Books, 1973.

Mahon, John K. *History of the Second Seminole War.* Gainesville: The University of Florida Press, 1973.

ACTIVITIES FOR "AN UNCONQUERED INDIAN"

Answer all questions on a separate sheet of paper.

Historical Understanding

Answer briefly:

1. When did the Seminole Indians first settle in Florida?

2. What were two causes of war between the United States and Indians of the Southeast?

3. To what were the inhabitants of Florida entitled according to the 1819 treaty between Spain and the United States?

4. During the administration of President Andrew Jackson what was the policy of the United States toward Indians in the southeastern states?

5. How did the Treaty of Moultrie Creek differ from the Treaty of Payne's Landing?

Reviewing the Facts of the Case

Answer briefly:

1. How did Osceola react to the Treaty of Moultrie Creek?

2. What was Osceola's response to the Treaty of Payne's Landing?

3. How did Osceola gain his release from the guardhouse at Fort King?

4. Why was Seminole Chief Charley Emathla killed?

5. What were the circumstances of Osceola's capture near St. Augustine?

Analyzing Ethical Issues

There is agreement about the answer to some questions. For other questions there is disagreement or uncertainty about the answer. We call these latter questions issues. Issues can be categorized as factual or ethical. A factual issue asks whether something is true or false, accurate or inaccurate. An ethical issue asks whether something is right or wrong, fair or unfair. Factual issues ask what *is*, ethical issues ask what *ought to be*.

For each of the following questions decide whether the issue is factual or ethical, as illustrated in this example:

Did the chiefs who signed the Moultrie Creek Treaty represent the wishes of most Seminoles? *Factual.*

Was Osceola justified in taking the life of General Wiley Thompson? *Ethical.*

1. Were runaway slaves treated as equals by the Seminoles?

2. Did the United States honor the terms of its treaty with Spain?

3. Should the U.S. government have forced the Seminoles to return fugitive slaves to their masters?

4. Were the Seminoles able to produce enough food on the Florida reservation to prevent starvation?

5. Should Osceola have punished Seminoles who stole food from whites outside the reservation?

6. Was General Wiley Thompson right to place Osceola in irons and lock him up in the Fort King guardhouse?

7. Was it fair of Seminole warriors to attack civilian plantations during the Second Seminole War?

8. Why did Osceola refuse to escape from his prison cell at Fort Marion?

Expressing Your Reasoning

1. After their argument in his office, General Wiley Thompson had Osceola placed in irons and locked up. To gain his release, Osceola agreed to emigrate west and urge his people to accept removal. Was it right of Osceola to lie to Thompson? Why or why not?

2. Many believed that General Jessup's capture of Osceola under a white flag of truce was an act of treachery. Jessup believed that he did the right thing. Write a paragraph in which you explain whether you think Jessup acted rightly or wrongly. Respond to the following points in your paragraph:
   a. A flag of truce is a recognized symbol that has been respected during wartime.
   b. Osceola had deceived whites before, and Jessup was doing the same thing in return.
   c. By capturing Osceola, Jessup was getting even with Osceola for making him look foolish once before. Earlier Osceola had carried out a surprise rescue of captured Indian prisoners under Jessup's control.
   d. By capturing Osceola, Jessup could strike a decisive blow against Seminole resistance and shorten the war.

   e. Almost all Florida whites approved of what Jessup had done.
   f. Osceola would never agree to a peace that required return of
      runaway slaves and removal of Seminoles from Florida.

3. The Seminoles believed that land could not be owned in the white
   man's sense of personal ownership. They believed that God allowed
   the Indian to use the land. In their view, land was sacred and could
   not be sold. Who do you think was entitled to own the land in
   Florida during the 1830s? Explain your position.

4. Should Osceola have escaped from his cell at Fort Marion when
   he had the opportunity? Why or why not?

5. *Seeking Additional Information.* In making decisions about such
   questions as those above, we often feel we need more information
   before we are satisfied with our judgments. Choose one of the
   above questions about which you would want more information
   than is presented in the story. What additional information would
   you like? Why would that information help you make a more
   satisfactory decision?

The Collapse of
Brotherly Love

PHILADELPHIA ETHNIC RIOTS

(Courtesy of the Library of Congress)

Riot in Philadelphia, June 7, 1844

Philadelphia is known as the City of Brotherly Love. In the 1840s, however, it was more a city of hate than love. A series of riots in 1844 led some to wonder if peace and order would ever return.

The tensions that exploded into violence had been growing for many years. Hostility between Protestants and Catholics was one of the major causes of the rioting. In particular there was hostility between *nativists* (Protestants who had been born in the United States) and the Catholics who had recently arrived from Ireland.

In the 1830s and 1840s, thousands of Irish immigrants came to the United States. In 1842, for example, about fifty thousand entered the country. Most of the immigrants had been small farmers in the Irish countryside, but, upon arrival, they tended to settle in Boston, New York, Philadelphia, and other cities. In 1844, the Irish were about 10 percent of the Philadelphia population of over three hundred thousand.

The nativists did not welcome the new immigrants. The immigrants were usually poor, some arriving without a penny. They often clustered together in certain parts of the city, which became known as tough Irish neighborhoods. Also, the Irish were Catholics, a religion that nativists distrusted.

Some resented the immigrants for economic reasons. Philadelphia was no longer the wealthy city it had been. Textile factories in New England could produce goods more cheaply than the hand-weavers of Philadelphia. The seaport of New York City was taking away much of the shipping business that had flourished in Philadelphia. The Philadelphia economy was in poor shape.

Because of their poverty, most of the immigrants were willing to work for low wages. Other workers claimed that cheap immigrant labor was making it difficult to get good-paying jobs.

Nativists also objected to the immigrants for political reasons. According to law, males born in the United States could vote after reaching the age of 21. Immigrants, however, could become citizens after a period of 5 years. They too, could not vote until the age of 21. Nativists argued that if a native-born American had to wait 21 years to vote, why should immigrants only have to wait 5 years?

In addition to these factors there was religious hostility and mis-understanding. Nativists were suspicious of the loyalty of the Catholics. They believed that Catholics were more loyal to the Pope than to the United States. Some nativists believed the Pope might call for a revolution, replacing democracy with monarchy. They believed Catholic priests would help organize such a revolution.

Conflict arose over how religion was treated in the public schools. For years public school children had sung Protestant hymns, said Protestant prayers, and read from the Protestant Bible—the King James version. Catholics opposed these practices. The law did not require children to attend schools, but if parents wanted their children to be educated, they had to attend public school. There were very few Catholic schools in Philadelphia at that time.

Francis Patrick Kenrick, the bishop of Philadelphia, opposed the way religion was treated in the public schools. There were Protestant religious practices and anti-Catholic textbooks. Catholics feared their young children were getting improper religious ideas in the schools. Catholics also believed that, because they paid taxes to help support the schools, schools should not be anti-Catholic in their practices.

Bishop Kenrick thought it was wrong that Catholic children were forced to participate in Protestant religious activities. In an 1842 letter to school officials he asked that Catholic children not be required to engage in Protestant religious exercises and that they be allowed to use the official Catholic Bible, the Douay version. That Bible contained notes giving the Catholic interpretation of Biblical passages.

In January 1843, the school board passed two resolutions. The first said that children would not be required to read the Bible if their parents objected. The second said that children could have any Bible of their choice as long as it was "without note or comment." The addition of that final statement meant the Douay version could not be chosen because it had notes.

Although Catholic children could now be excused from class during the reading of the Protestant Bible, they could not bring their own. The bishop was discouraged. The board had taken only a tiny step in the right direction.

Many nativists believed the board had gone too far. They became convinced that the Catholics intended to get rid of the Bible in schools. Excusing Catholic children from Bible reading was a step in the wrong direction. They said it could lead to elimination of any religious instruction in the schools.

Anti-Catholic feelings grew stronger. A Protestant teacher in

Kensington ignored the board's ruling about excusing Catholic children from Bible reading. The school director, a Catholic, ordered her to follow the board's rule. Soon more rumors spread that Catholics were trying to eliminate the Bible.

At public meetings, nativist speakers gave long anti-Catholic talks. A nativist political party, the American Republican party, used the Bible issue to rally support. Anti-immigrant and anti-Catholic writings appeared in many nativist newspapers.

Conditions for Catholic children in the schools remained unchanged. In March 1844, Bishop Kenrick again wrote to the school board. In an effort to stop the nativist uproar, he also wrote a letter to the citizens of Philadelphia. In the letter, which appeared in newspapers and was posted throughout the city, he explained that Catholics did not want to get rid of the Bible. Catholics wanted "liberty of conscience," and that meant they wanted to use their version of the Bible.

The unrest created by the Bible issue increased. The American Republican party continued to organize. In the 1844 election many of their candidates were elected. The party even decided to try to organize in Irish sections of the city. In Kensington, local Irish groups threatened to destroy any house in which an American Republican party meeting was held.

On May 3, an open meeting in a vacant Kensington lot ended in a brawl between local Irish toughs and some of the nativists. The party scheduled another meeting for Monday the sixth. They urged party members from throughout the state to attend. About three thousand people came. The mood was ugly. One local Irishman dumped a load of dirt, some said it was manure, in front of the speakers' stand.

As the meeting began, a heavy rain began. The crowd ran to a nearby market building for shelter. There was a group of Irish in the building and soon a fight broke out. Gunfire erupted from nearby Irish houses and one nativist, 18-year-old George Schiffler, was killed.

After fleeing the area, a number of nativists returned and more gunfire was exchanged. Finally, the sheriff, Morton McMichael, and his men arrived and the fighting stopped.

There had been many instances of mob violence in past years, but this was the first in which guns were used extensively. It had been a common understanding that guns should not be used.

There was no organized professional police force in Philadelphia. The sheriff had to rely on volunteers for his troops, and they were not allowed to carry guns. Only the state militia could carry guns.

McMichael asked General George Cadwalder, commander of the nearby militia, for help. Cadwalder refused because he could only act if so ordered by the governor.

Things got worse. The next morning a nativist newspaper wrote: "The bloody hand of the Pope has stretched forth to our destruction. . . . Our liberties are now to be fought for—let us not be slack in our preparation."

Thousands attended a meeting behind Independence Hall. Some of the speakers urged the nativist crowd to protest, but not to use violence. Other speakers gave anti-Catholic and anti-immigrant speeches. A mood of revenge was in the air. There was talk of burning the Irish Catholic churches.

Bishop Kenrick was distressed. Some Catholics wanted to have permission to obtain guns to protect the churches. The bishop opposed that idea, believing it would provoke more violence. A number of his friends also urged him to leave the city for his own safety. Reluctantly he agreed, and left the city for a few days.

On Tuesday there was more violence in Kensington. Many houses were burned and more gunfire exchanged. This time the militia was permitted to assist Sheriff McMichael in dispersing the mobs. Hundreds of Irish families left the area.

The next afternoon the mobs returned. Some soldiers from the militia were protecting St. Michael's Church. These troops were lured away by fires started in nearby buildings. Then the mob attacked the church and set it afire. The crowd cheered as the church burned down. That evening another church, St. Augustine's, was also burned.

New powers were given to the militia. In the past, soldiers could be sued for any damages they caused when establishing order. That policy was changed. Also troops were given permission to shoot to kill if necessary to control the mobs.

For a time the violence ended. In June an investigating grand jury, dominated by Protestants, issued a report blaming the violence on the Catholics for trying to get the Bible out of the schools. In addition, the jury said the American Republican party had a right to hold public meetings.

The American Republican party officially condemned the violence. They said it was started by rowdy teenagers and outlaws.

A Catholic group wrote a lengthy response to the grand jury report. They said the violence did not begin until Irish homes were attacked. They said the first shots were fired in self-defense. They also wrote that their rights to freedom of religion were violated by the way religion was treated in the schools.

The Catholic responses did not ease the tensions. There was fear of more violence because the American Republican party was planning a huge Fourth of July parade. It was clear that nativist opinions were going to be glorified in the parade. There was the danger that the emotions aroused might lead to more rioting.

Fear of violence led William Dunn, the brother of the pastor of St. Phillip's Church, to speak to the governor. He asked Governor Porter for permission to have guns to protect the church. The governor agreed and gave Dunn 20 muskets. The public did not know of this action; neither did Bishop Kenrick.

The parade featured many anti-Catholic signs portraying the end of Catholic power. A large nativist meeting was held after the parade, but there was no violence that night.

The next day guns were seen being taken into St. Phillip's. A rumor quickly spread that the Catholics were planning to attack the nativists. That night a mob surrounded the church. Sheriff McMichael was unable to disperse the crowd, but the church was not attacked.

On Sunday the mob returned. They brought a cannon and fired it at the church. The militia arrived, and, in the confusion and excitement, the troops were ordered to fire. Throughout Sunday night troops and nativists fought through the dark streets. At least ten people were killed and many wounded.

On Monday, Governor Porter arrived with 5,800 soldiers. The troops stayed in the city for a month. There was no more bloodshed.

Although the nativist American Republican party denied supporting the violence, many citizens blamed them for what happened. The party lost strength and was no longer a major force in Philadelphia politics.

To relax tensions, Bishop Kenrick ordered Pastor Dunn to leave the city. The bishop, believing the school policies would not change, began a program of opening private Catholic schools. Philadelphia soon had one of the largest parochial school systems in the country.

In later years, partly as a result of the 1844 riots, Philadelphia organized a professional police force and found a way to maintain law and order.

The major sources for this story were:

Feldberg, Michael. *The Philadelphia Riots of 1844*. Westport, Conn.: Greenwood Press, 1975.
Nolan, Hugh, J. *The Most Reverend Francis Patrick Kenrick, Third Bishop of Philadelphia, 1830–1851*. Philadelphia: American Catholic Historical Society of Philadelphia, 1948.

ACTIVITIES FOR "THE COLLAPSE OF BROTHERLY LOVE"

Answer all questions on a separate sheet of paper.

Historical Understanding

Answer briefly:

1. Identify three reasons why immigrants were often resented.
2. What position did nativists take regarding religion in the schools and the right to vote?
3. In what ways did school practices offend Catholics?
4. What were two long-term effects of the riots?

Reviewing the Facts of the Case

Answer briefly:

1. What did Bishop Kenrick request of the school board?
2. What was the school board's response to the bishop's request?
3. How did violence first begin?
4. According to the grand jury, what caused the Kensington riots?
5. What did William Dunn ask of the governor?

Analyzing Ethical Issues

There are many incidents in this story involving the following values:

LIBERTY: a value concerning what freedoms people should have and the limits that may justifiably be placed upon them.

AUTHORITY: a value concerning what rules or people should be obeyed and the consequences for disobedience.

EQUALITY: a value concerning whether people should be treated in the same way.

TRUTH: a value concerning the expression, distortion, or withholding of accurate information.

LIFE: a value concerning when, if ever, it is justifiable to threaten or take the life of another.

Choose *three* of the above values and describe an incident in which it was involved, as illustrated in this example:

The value of truth was involved in William Dunn's secret request for weapons because he didn't tell Bishop Kenrick about it.

Expressing Your Reasoning

1. Bishop Kenrick did not want guns to be used to defend the churches. He said, "Rather let every church burn than shed one drop of blood or imperil one precious soul." The bishop of New York City seemed to disagree. He said, "The people should have defended the churches." Should Bishop Kenrick have allowed his people to use guns to defend the churches? Why or why not?

2. The way religion was treated in the schools offended the Catholic community. Bishop Kenrick wanted Catholic students to be able to use their own Bible and to be kept away from Protestant activities and anti-Catholic books. What would have been a fair way for the school board to have treated Bible readings in the schools? Write a paragraph explaining your answer to the question.

3. *Seeking Additional Information.* In making decisions about such questions as those above, we often feel we need more information before we are satisfied with our judgments. Choose one of the above questions about which you would want more information than is presented in the story. What additional information would you like? Why would that information help you make a more satisfactory decision?

A Different Drummer

HENRY DAVID THOREAU

(*Courtesy, U.S. Postal Service*)

U.S. Postage Stamp Issued in 1967,
Commemorating Thoreau's 150th Birthday

"If a man does not keep pace with his companions, perhaps it is because he hears a different drummer. Let him step to the music which he hears, however measured, or far away." These words were written by a U.S. rebel and literary giant, Henry David Thoreau. His opinions of the society around him during the 1830s and 1840s were highly critical. He was not fond of the spread of factories and railroads in the North, or the expansion of slavery in the South. Thoreau deplored what he considered the greed and materialism of his times. What disturbed him most of all were events in the fastest growing section of the new nation, the West.

As the frontier pushed farther and farther west, Americans came to believe in what they termed their *manifest destiny*. Originally this term represented a desire to spread democratic government to all people of the western hemisphere. By the 1830s manifest destiny had taken on a slightly different meaning. According to many land-hungry Americans of the time it was the destiny or historic duty of the United States to expand westward to the Pacific Ocean. Manifest destiny was soon to collide with the Mexican border.

During the 1820s a democratic government in Mexico opened its land to U.S. settlers. By 1830 more than twenty thousand Americans, many of them Southerners, had entered Texas, at this time a part of Mexico. Although slavery had been outlawed in Mexico, many settlers brought their slaves with them anyway.

In 1830 Mexico closed its doors to further settlement. A new military government feared the growth of a U.S. state in Texas. Americans in Texas protested the new policy vigorously. Fighting broke out in 1835. The Mexican Army besieged a force of 180 Texans in an old Spanish mission called the Alamo. The Texans died to a man while defending the mission. Soon thereafter, another force of Texans rallied behind the leadership of Sam Houston. Under the cry "Remember the Alamo," the Texans defeated the leading Mexican general at the Battle of San Jacinto.

Meanwhile, in March 1836 a group of Texans declared their independence from Mexico. They drafted a constitution for a new republic of Texas, often called the Lone Star Republic. The United States recognized the new government, but Mexico did not.

When the new republic petitioned to join the United States, strong opposition developed. Since Texas allowed slavery, Northerners in Congress opposed admission of another slave state to the Union. Others feared that to admit Texas would lead to war with Mexico.

The Democratic presidential candidate of 1844, James K. Polk, called for the annexation of Texas. Soon after his election, Texas was admitted to the Union. The annexation of Texas was a blow to the Mexican national pride as well as a loss of territory and touched off a war with Mexico (1846–1848). Mexico feared that events in Texas were only the beginning of an attempt by the United States to win control of the entire Southwest.

Some Northerners were opposed to the war against Mexico. They feared that slavery would spread into the vast area that might be acquired as a result of the conflict. One concern of the opponents was that, in the future, there might be a majority of slave states in the Senate. This would reduce the chance that the federal government could prevent the spread of slavery. One of the Northern opponents of the war was Henry David Thoreau.

Henry was born in Concord, Massachusetts in 1817 and resided there nearly his entire life. His father made pencils for a living. His mother often kept boarders in the family house where Henry heard abolitionist (anti-slavery) views expressed at the dinner table. Henry had a brother and two sisters. The Thoreau family enjoyed an affectionate home life. None of the four children ever married or moved away.

Although Henry's boyhood home was in Concord Village, he cherished the countryside surrounding the village. As a child he was attracted to the out-of-doors and the companionship of nature. He was homesick when away from Concord. In a letter to his mother, written from New York, he said, "I would be content to sit in Concord, under the poplar tree, henceforth, forever."

He graduated from nearby Harvard at age 20. In college he was just a village boy away from home. He was not much impressed by the school, nor did he make much of an impression upon his professors. His life there was solitary and dull, but he loved the library. Though far from the top of his class, Henry was probably the most well-read Harvard graduate of 1837.

In a college essay Thoreau expressed his growing dislike of conformity. The essay urged independent thought and strong individuality. "The fear of displeasing the world," he wrote, "ought not in the least to influence my actions." He remained a nonconformist his whole life.

After college Thoreau was troubled by how to make a living without sacrificing his individuality. He became a teacher in the

Concord Public Elementary School. One day, while observing his class, a member of the school committee noticed that Thoreau did not flog his pupils when they did poorly in school. After class, he was ordered to begin using the cowhide switch on his pupils.

Thoreau believed that physical punishment had no relation to good education. To express his view that physical punishment was senseless, he thrashed six good students and resigned.

Later, Thoreau and his older brother, John, opened a successful private school in Concord. No flogging was allowed. Emphasis was placed on nature study. In their school the Thoreau brothers introduced "field trips." They often took students boating on the river and had them search for arrowheads, birds, and flowers.

The private school closed in 1841 because of John's ill health, and Thoreau was again troubled about how to support himself. He earned some income manufacturing pencils with his father. This work, however, did not leave Thoreau the freedom he wanted to study nature and write.

Around this time Thoreau made the acquaintance of Ralph Waldo Emerson, who also lived in Concord. Emerson was a world-famous scholar, 14 years older than Thoreau. The two developed a lasting relationship.

Emerson was the leader of a group of Concord thinkers known as the *transcendentalists*. Their first principle was freedom of thought. The group's favorite meeting place was Emerson's house. Thoreau joined the group. Emerson saw in Thoreau an undeveloped genius. It was in Emerson's company that Thoreau's mind came alive.

The transcendentalists were optimistic that a new American mind would emerge. They urged people to be self-reliant—stand on their own feet, free themselves from ignorance, and think for themselves. They believed that free of dead European ideas, the new American would discover eternal truths.

According to the transcendentalists, discovery of those truths required a fresh approach to human knowledge. They abandoned the prevailing European theory that held that all knowledge is gained through the senses—from touch, sight, hearing, taste, and smell.

The transcendentalists believed differently. According to them there was a body of knowledge within every person that goes beyond (transcends) the senses. This knowledge was the voice of God within a human being. For each person this divine knowledge was a conscience, a moral sense, an inner light.

Emerson not only influenced Thoreau's thinking, but also helped him support himself. Thoreau agreed to work as a handyman around the Emerson household and to tutor Emerson's son in exchange for a room and meals in the Emerson house.

Thoreau fell in love with a young woman, Ellen Sewall, and proposed marriage to her. She refused him. Thereafter his romantic feelings were channeled into a deep love of nature. Thoreau was married to the woods, water, and wilderness of New England.

Living and working at the Emerson household failed to provide Thoreau the solitude he craved. He took delight in his daily walks in the woods, but he wanted more privacy than he could get living at the Emersons'.

As he wandered through the village or its surroundings Thoreau was often mistaken for a farmer. His boots were never polished and his clothes were homespun. He ridiculed the manners of polite Concord society. Many in the Concord community considered him an eccentric loner or even a shiftless crank. He scoffed at their acquisitions of material possessions. In his quest to simplify life, material belongings had little importance. The mass of men, he said, lived "lives of quiet desperation" struggling to get rich and buy things.

He finally thought of a plan to support himself and provide both privacy and simplicity. He decided to escape to Walden Pond, located on property owned by Emerson. He went there, he said, "to live deliberately, to confront only the essential facts of life, and see if I could not learn what it had to teach, and not, when I came to die, discover that I had not lived."

With his own hands he built a cabin near the pond. Into it he moved a bed, a desk, a table, a few utensils, three chairs, and a tiny mirror. He also planted a small vegetable garden. Here he would live on his own terms. For two years he lived like a hermit at Walden studying the natural environment and recording his thoughts at great length in a journal.

At Walden, Thoreau accepted his animal neighbors as they accepted him. In his journal he reported that a mouse nested under his cabin and came to pick crumbs at his feet while he ate lunch.

Thoreau believed that it was wrong to take the life of any creature that breathed. Because of this belief, he had a strong preference for a vegetarian diet. He did catch fish now and then, but felt guilty about it.

One day he discovered that woodchucks were destroying beans in his Walden garden. He caught one in a metal trap and then let it go.

The same woodchuck reappeared in his garden a few days later and was again trapped. When Thoreau asked a visitor to his cabin what he should do with the woodchuck, the reply was "knock his brains out." Thoreau carried the woodchuck two miles away, opened the trap, and set him free.

While at Walden it was unusual for Thoreau to pay attention to what went on very far from Concord. The Mexican War, however, spurred him to protest. In late July 1846, just as the blueberries were getting ripe, Henry walked one evening from Walden into Concord. He was on his way to get a mended shoe from the cobbler's. In the village he was stopped by Sam Staples, the local constable, tax collector, and jailer.

Thoreau had not paid his poll tax for three years and owed $1.50. The poll tax was levied on all eligible voters. Staples insisted that Thoreau pay the tax due. Thoreau refused to pay the tax to the state. It was a state, he said, that buys and sells men, women, and children, referring to slaves.

Staples pleaded with Thoreau to pay the tax. Thoreau said, "If you call on me to pay for a rifle, Sam, it's the same as asking me to fire it. You're making me as much a killer as a foot soldier, who crashed the border into faraway Mexico." Sam thereupon locked Thoreau up in the Concord jail.

The Mexican War had stiffened Thoreau's opposition to the poll tax. In his words: "When a sixth of the population of a nation which has undertaken to be the refuge of liberty are slaves, and a whole country is unjustly overrun and conquered by a foreign army . . . I think it is not too soon for honest men to rebel."

The morning after he was jailed, Thoreau's aunt paid the tax without his consent, and he was released from jail. A short time afterward he met Emerson, who thought Thoreau had acted in bad taste by refusing to pay the tax. When they met, Emerson, referring to jail, said, "Henry, why were you in there?" Henry's reply was "Why were you *not* in there?"

Two years after the night he spent in jail Thoreau explained his defiance of the law in an essay. The title of that essay, *Civil Disobedience*, has become an important concept in political history. In the essay Thoreau tries to justify peaceful resistance by citizens to the authority of government. Some of the lasting ideas from this essay include:

1. "To be patriots, some citizens must serve the state with their consciences and resist the government."
2. "If [an injustice of the government] . . . requires you to be an agent of injustice to another, then, I say break the law."

Thoreau was again aroused to civil disobedience during the early 1850s. In 1850, Congress passed the Fugitive Slave Law. The law granted slaveholders, or their agents, authority to seize and carry back to the South runaway slaves found in the North. Under the law local citizens were prohibited from aiding runaways and could be ordered by a court to join a posse to catch fugitive slaves. In Boston, a runaway had been sent back to slavery in early 1851 by Massachusetts authorities.

On September 30, 1851, Henry Williams, who had escaped from slavery in Virginia to Boston, learned there were warrants out for his arrest. He fled on foot to Concord where he sought out the Thoreau family. They lodged the fugitive for the night and collected funds to help him along the way. The next morning Henry Thoreau went to the railroad station and bought a ticket for the runaway. By helping him get safely on his way to Canada, Thoreau risked prosecution for breaking federal law. There was also the danger of slave-catchers who would often use violence to recapture a runaway.

In 1862, Henry David Thoreau, age 44, fell victim to tuberculosis. He died as he lived—one of the freest Americans. He was buried in Sleepy Hollow Cemetery on the woody knolls that were his pleasure in Concord. His ideas about personal freedom were not laid to rest with their author. Among others, Leo Tolstoy in his opposition to czarist Russia, Mohandas Gandhi in his resistance to British rule in India, and Martin Luther King in his struggle for the civil rights of black Americans all expressed a debt to Thoreau's concept of civil disobedience.

The major sources for this story were:

Canaby, Henry S. *Thoreau*. Boston: Houghton Mifflin, 1939.

Connor, Seymour V., and Faulk, Odie B. *North America Divided: The Mexican War 1846-1848*. New York: Oxford University Press, 1971.

Derleth, August. *Concord Rebel: A Life of Henry D. Thoreau*. Philadelphia: Chilton, 1962.

Harding, Walter. *The Days of Henry Thoreau*. New York: Alfred A. Knopf, 1966.

Thoreau, Henry D. *Walden and Civil Disobedience*. New York: W.W. Norton, 1966.

ACTIVITIES FOR "A DIFFERENT DRUMMER"

Answer all questions on a separate sheet of paper.

Historical Understanding

Answer briefly:

1. What did *manifest destiny* mean to nineteenth-century Americans?

2. What provoked war between the United States and Mexico?

3. Why were some Northerners opposed to the Mexican War?

4. What were the major provisions of the Fugitive Slave Law of 1850?

Reviewing the Facts of the Case

Answer briefly:

1. Why did Sam Staples arrest Thoreau?

2. After his release from jail what did Thoreau reply to Emerson's question: "Why were you in there?" What do you think Thoreau meant by his reply?

3. How did Thoreau justify going to jail?

4. What did Thoreau do when Henry Williams arrived in Concord?

Analyzing Ethical Issues

Sometimes people face situations in which values are in conflict. There are several places in this story in which *authority* (a value concerning what rules or people should be obeyed) comes into conflict with *liberty* (a value concerning what freedoms people should have and the limits that may justifiably be placed on them). For example, the values of authority and liberty were in conflict when the Texans proclaimed their independence from the rule of Mexico.

Identify and write down two other situations in this story where the values of authority and liberty are in conflict.

Expressing Your Reasoning

1. Should Thoreau have paid his poll tax? Why or why not?

2. Emerson disagreed with Thoreau's refusal to pay the poll tax. He believed that Thoreau should try to bring about reform within the framework of the laws. Below are several reasons opposed to Thoreau's decision. Explain which of the following you think is the best reason for Thoreau to have paid his poll tax. Which do you think is the worst reason? Why?

   a. The amount of the tax ($1.50) was small and Thoreau could afford to pay it.
   b. If he paid the tax Thoreau would not have to go to jail and could return to his Walden cabin.
   c. By paying the tax Thoreau would have prevented his family from being embarrassed.
   d. Thoreau's protest was ineffective. Going to jail didn't persuade anyone to oppose either the Mexican War or slavery.
   e. By going to jail Thoreau was trying to get attention for himself and causing unnecessary trouble.
   f. Thoreau was breaking the law by refusing to pay his poll tax. Good citizens ought to support their government by obeying the law and paying their taxes.
   g. A majority of Americans supported the war with Mexico. In a democracy citizens ought to comply with the rule of the majority.

3. The transcendentalists believed that a conscience was the divine presence in every person. What do you think a conscience is? Is conscience the best basis for deciding what is right or wrong? Write a paragraph answering these questions.

4. Thoreau preferred to be a vegetarian. He believed that no one should take the life of a creature that breathed. Do animals have a right to life? Explain your position.

5. Should Thoreau have helped the fugitive slave, Henry Williams, escape to Canada? Why or why not?

6. *Seeking Additional Information.* In making decisions about such questions as those above, we often feel we need more information before we are satisfied with our judgments. Choose one of the above questions about which you would want more information

than is presented in the story. What additional information would
you like? How would that information help you make a more
satisfactory decision?

PART 3

A House Divided

(1850–1876)

You Can't Hold Still

PETER STILL

(*Courtesy of the Library of Congress*)

Slave in Chains

It was a hot Sunday afternoon in Maryland sometime in the early 1800s. Six-year-old Peter and his eight-year-old brother, Levin, were playing in the summer sun. The boys thought their parents were at church. A horse-drawn buggy pulled up. The driver gave the boys some cake and told them to jump in. He said their mother wanted them to come to a party. The children were uncertain but finally agreed. They climbed aboard and were driven away. Levin would never see his parents again, and it would be almost fifty years before Peter would again see his mother.

Peter and Levin were black children, the sons of slave parents. They had been kidnapped by the man in the buggy. He took them to Lexington, Kentucky, and sold them into slavery. The Fisher family paid $150 for each of the boys.

Little Peter and Levin were frightened. They deeply missed their family. Peter told Mr. Fisher that they had been kidnapped. Fisher knocked Peter to the floor and beat him. He told Peter never to say he had been stolen. If people knew that the boys had been stolen, Fisher would have trouble getting a good price if he decided to sell them.

Fisher's son sympathized with the boys and tried to persuade his father to be more understanding. Mr. Fisher screamed at his son and made him promise never to talk to anyone about the boys being stolen.

Later, Fisher's son whispered to Peter that he knew a man named Henry Clay, a prominent United States senator, who lived nearby. He thought that Clay could help Peter get free from the Fishers. Secretly the boys went to Senator Clay and told him their story. Clay said he would see what he could do, and the boys' hopes were raised. Their hopes were not realized, however.

An old slave woman tried to teach Peter a lesson in slave survival. She told him never to trust white people, to tell whites what they wanted to hear, and to always seem happy. She taught him a song with the words: "Got one mind for the boss to see, / Got another mind for what I know is me."

Peter and Levin worked in Fisher's brickyard. One of the bosses of the yard was also a slave. He had power over the other slaves. If he thought one of the slaves was not working properly, he could have that slave beaten. One day Peter was ordered to whip another slave. Peter was terrified. How could he whip another person? The boss told

Peter that if he failed to lay on the whip, then he himself would be beaten. Peter began to whip the slave, but he could not keep it up. Sick to his stomach at the sight of the bloody wounds, he ran crying from the brickyard. The slave boss laughed, but never ordered Peter to do any more beatings.

One day Peter and Levin heard bad news. Fisher had decided to move to Cincinnati and to leave them behind. Fisher had been a relatively kind master, and his slaves were usually well fed and decently clothed. Peter and Levin were sold to Nat Gist. Gist was known as a cruel man who, while drunk, often beat his slaves.

Gist's reputation was deserved. The first week Peter was there, he was whipped severely for feeding a horse improperly. The cowhide whip cut deep wounds in his back. Peter vowed that he would not be whipped again. He worked hard and became Gist's favorite slave.

One day Gist shouted out in disgust. Two white men had set up a Sunday school where they were teaching slaves how to read and write. Gist angrily told Peter: "Any of *my* property goes near that school, and he'll get such a flogging he'll never need any more education or anything else. You understand me, boy?" Peter said he understood.

The next Sunday, Peter secretly went to the school. If he could learn to read and write, maybe he could send letters to the North and find his family. Maybe he and Levin could free themselves at last.

At school the teacher told Peter that he had to have written permission from his master allowing him to attend school. Peter told the teacher that his master had urged him to come to the school and that everything was all right. The teacher allowed Peter to stay that day but told him he would have to bring a pass the next time.

That night Peter told Levin about the school. Levin warned Peter not to go. If Gist found out, Peter would certainly be beaten. Nonetheless, Peter was not afraid.

The next Sunday he returned to the school. Again the teacher asked for his pass, and again Peter said his master had given permission. The teacher allowed Peter to stay but explained the problem again. In Lexington slaves could attend school only if they had a pass from their masters. If anyone found out Peter was attending school without a pass, the school would be closed down and no one would be able to learn.

Peter did not want the school to close, but he wanted to learn. The next Sunday he told the teacher that his master was on a trip and therefore could not write out the pass. The teacher began to realize that Peter was lying. Sadly, he told Peter that he would have to leave. Peter glumly returned home.

In 1818, Nat Gist died. In his will he left his property to his nephew, Levi Gist. Because they were slaves, Peter and Levin were treated like any other piece of property. Levi Gist became their new owner. The boys were somewhat pleased because Levi was known as a kind man. Unfortunately, they were saddened to learn that they were being taken to a tiny town in Alabama where Levi planned to live.

Peter and Levin dreamed of freedom. Many slaves had escaped from their masters; many others tried and failed. If an escaping slave was caught, the punishment was severe. The slave would be beaten and possibly mutilated or killed. Peter and Levin decided that running away was too risky.

Peter had heard of another way to become free—he himself might be able to buy his freedom. Slaves were sometimes allowed to work at paying jobs after their daily duties were finished. Whenever he could, Peter took such jobs and saved the small amount of money he earned. Someday, he hoped, he would have a master who would be willing to sell Peter to himself!

It was not easy to buy oneself. It took a long time to earn enough money. Also, he would have to have a master he could trust. He knew of a slave who worked and saved for years because his master promised the slave could buy himself. When the slave had earned $1,000, the master took the money and sold the slave to a new owner. Peter would have to be careful.

Peter continued to work and save. Then, one day, on a nearby plantation he met Vina. Vina was a new slave woman of the McKiernan family. She was beautiful and kind. Soon, she and Peter fell in love.

Peter was now in his early twenties. He still longed for freedom, but now he had another problem: he also loved Vina. If they were married, he would have a new responsibility. It would be hard enough to earn money to buy himself, but it would be almost impossible to buy his wife as well. He tried to forget Vina, but he could not. On June 25, 1825, he and Vina were married.

Because they were owned by different people, Peter and Vina could not live together. They were allowed to see each other only when their daily work was done and on Sundays. Peter worked hard to make his new wife happy. He built a cabin for her and used his savings to buy needed goods. Soon he had another responsibility. Vina gave birth to a son whom they named Peter. Later she had another son whom they named Levin.

Peter still wanted freedom, but his hope was fading. In 1832, his brother Levin died. Now Peter had no one to talk to about the old days with his mother and father. Peter finally recovered from his sadness, and his inner strength returned. He was determined to buy his way to freedom. Once he got North he would try to earn enough money to buy his family their freedom. It would take years of struggle, but he believed being free was worth the effort.

After Gist's death, Peter had a new owner named Hogun. Peter pretended to have a bad back and said he could not work well in the fields. Hogun decided to rent Peter's labor to other people in the town who would then pay Hogun for Peter's services.

One man Peter worked for owned a bookstore. There was not much to do, so the owner said that Peter could take other jobs when he was finished in the store. He said Peter could keep the money he earned, but that it had to be kept a secret. It was against the law for Peter to earn money for himself while he was working as a rented slave.

Peter took various jobs, which included polishing shoes, working in a hotel, and cleaning classrooms at a school. One day he met Isaac and Joseph Friedman. The Friedmans were German Jews who had come to the United States and had established a dry goods business. They owned a store and sold cloth to the people in the area. They were the first Jews to live in the area, and local townspeople were suspicious of them. At first Peter was suspicious also, but he soon came to trust them.

Peter began to work for the Friedmans. They were kind to him and paid him twice as much as he usually earned. Peter thought that if the Friedmans were his owners they might sell him his freedom. The trouble was he was owned by Hogun.

Peter developed a plan. The Friedmans' business was doing well, and they wanted to hire Peter for a year. Peter was now 45 years old, and he continued to fake back pains when Mr. Hogun was around. He also began faking a bad cough. He wanted to convince Hogun that he was sickly. Then, perhaps, Hogun would be willing to sell him to the Friedmans.

Peter began to trust the Friedmans more and more. He learned that Jews had once been slaves, so he thought the Friedmans would be sympathetic. He had been warned not to trust white people, but he decided to take a chance. He explained his plan to the Friedman brothers and they agreed to help him. If Hogun would sell Peter for $500, the amount Peter had been able to save, the Friedmans would in turn sell Peter to himself.

Peter continued coughing and complaining of a bad back. Hogun eventually agreed to sell him to the Friedmans. The Friedmans were true to their word and, at last, after over 40 years of being a slave, Peter "belonged" to himself.

His joy was short-lived. The Friedmans discovered that an 1833 Alabama law made it illegal to sell a slave his freedom without the permission of a judge. The Friedmans did not believe a judge would give permission. There was anti-Jewish feeling in the area, and the circumstances surrounding the sale would make the judge suspicious. The Friedmans thought the judge would probably rule the sale illegal.

Peter was stunned but did not give up. The Friedmans were planning to move to Cincinnati and they said Peter could come with them. They would pretend that Peter was their servant. It would be dangerous, because slave-catchers might steal him and return him to Alabama.

Peter explained to Vina that he was going to the North and would try to earn money to buy her and the children. He told his sons that they must not marry because it was not likely that Peter could earn enough money to buy additional slaves. It would be hard enough to buy his family as it was.

Peter was successful in his trip north. After leaving the Friedmans, he went to Philadelphia where, at an antislavery headquarters, he met a young black man named William Still. When Peter told him his story, William's heart jumped. His mother had told him that he had two older brothers who had been stolen before he was born. Peter was one of William's long-lost brothers!

At first, Peter was suspicious. He knew there were black people who made money turning in escaped slaves. He had to be careful that he was not being tricked. But this time all was well. Peter met the rest of his family. He learned that his last name was Still. Before this his last name had always been that of his most recent owner. His father had died, but his mother was still alive. With tears, prayers, and embraces, Peter was finally reunited with his mother.

Now, how to get his family out of slavery? It would take years to earn enough money, but it seemed the safest way. Then he met Seth Concklin. Concklin was a white man who hated slavery. He acted on his hatred by going to the South to help slaves escape. He had been successful in the past, but if he were caught, the punishment would be cruel.

In spite of the danger, Peter agreed to allow Concklin to try to get his family. Concklin went to Alabama and succeeded in helping Peter's family escape from the plantation. On their way north, however, they were captured by slave-catchers. Peter's family was returned to the McKiernans. His sons received 250 lashes with the whip. Vina received 100 lashes. Only his young daughter, Catherine, was not beaten. When Peter heard of this punishment, he was somewhat relieved, because he had feared it would be more severe.

Concklin's fate was much worse. His body was found in a river. He was wrapped in chains and his skull had been fractured.

Peter was heartbroken but would not quit. With the help of the Friedmans and others, negotiations began with McKiernan. McKiernan agreed to sell the family for $5,000.

Peter began working, but after one year he had only earned about $100. He could never earn enough to buy his family. Peter decided he would travel throughout the Northeast, telling his story in churches and at antislavery meetings. He hoped that people would be willing to donate money to help him.

His brother did not think it was a good idea. He said people probably would not give money just to help one family. So many others were equally bad off. Nonetheless, Peter decided to try.

Some people refused to give money just to help one family. They said they hated slavery so much they would not allow their money to go into the hands of any slaveholder. Peter continued his journey.

From 1852 to 1854 Peter traveled through New Jersey, New York, and New England. The money slowly built up. Harriet Beecher Stowe, William Lloyd Garrison, and other well-known *abolitionists* (those who wanted to end slavery) supported him and urged others to donate money. Finally, late in 1854, Peter had raised the $5,000.

Through an agent, Peter's money was taken to McKiernan. McKiernan released the family. In Cincinnati, Peter waited nervously as a steamboat pulled into the dock. Would his family really be on the boat? He looked at the crowd on the deck. His family was not in sight. Then they appeared. Vina, Peter, Levin, and Catherine all were there. They had a joyous reunion.

There was one note of sadness, however. Against his father's orders, young Peter had married. His wife had died, but his baby boy still lived. They had to leave him in Alabama. McKiernan would not include the baby in the price of the family.

Kate Pickard, a woman who had helped Peter raise money, wanted Peter and his family to help in the antislavery movement. She hoped they could show everyone the value of freedom. By publicizing their lives in writings and meetings, the Stills could help people see "if it pays to buy people out of slavery."

In spite of Pickard's pleas, Peter and his family refused to participate in antislavery efforts. Perhaps they feared for their own safety. Peter's mother had been a runaway slave, so her family might technically all be considered slaves under the law.

Peter and his family settled down and led quiet lives. Peter bought a small farm near Burlington, New Jersey. There he worked until his death in 1868. The Civil War had ended, and the Thirteenth Amendment was passed. Slavery had become illegal throughout the United States.

The major sources for this story were:

Mann, Peggy, and Siegal, Vivian W. *The Man Who Bought Himself*. New York: Macmillan, 1975.

Pickard, Kate E. *The Kidnapped and the Ransomed*. Facsimile edition of the 1856 book. Philadelphia: The Jewish Publication Society of America, 1970.

Toplin, Robert B. "Peter Still Versus the Peculiar Institution." *Civil War History*, December 1967, pp. 340–349.

ACTIVITIES FOR "YOU CAN'T HOLD STILL"

Answer all questions on a separate sheet of paper.

Historical Understanding

Answer briefly:

1. Describe two ways in which slaves were treated like property.

2. Why was it dangerous to help runaway slaves?

3. Identify two ways in which the law restricted slaves.

Reviewing the Facts of the Case

Answer briefly:

1. Why did Mr. Fisher tell the boys not to say they were stolen?
2. What advice did the old slave woman give to Peter?
3. Why did Peter's teacher demand a written pass?
4. Why were Peter and Levin afraid of running away?
5. Why was Peter reluctant to marry Vina? Why did he tell his sons not to marry?
6. Why did Peter fake illness in front of Mr. Hogun?
7. Why did the Friedmans think the sale of Peter to himself would be illegal?
8. What did Kate Pickard want the Stills to do?

Analyzing Ethical Issues

There are a number of incidents in this story involving the following values:

AUTHORITY: a value concerning what rules or people should be obeyed and the consequences for disobedience.

LIBERTY: a value concerning what freedoms people should have and the limits that may be justifiably placed upon them.

LIFE: a value concerning when, if ever, it is justifiable to threaten or take the life of another.

PROPERTY: a value concerning what people should be allowed to own and how they should be allowed to use it.

TRUTH: a value concerning the expression, distortion, or withholding of accurate information.

For each of the following incidents write a sentence indicating what value or values were involved, as illustrated in this example.

Fisher's son decided to tell Senator Clay about Peter. *The value of authority was involved because Mr. Fisher had ordered his son not to tell anyone that Peter had been stolen, and his son violated his father's authority.*

1. While on rental at the bookstore, Peter earned extra money at odd jobs.

2. Peter told his teacher that his master wanted him to go to school.

3. Peter told his sons not to marry.

4. Peter pretended he was sick.

5. Peter allowed Concklin to try to help his family escape.

6. The Friedmans sold Peter to himself.

7. When his family was freed, Peter did not help the abolitionists as they had asked.

Expressing Your Reasoning

1. Kate Pickard helped Peter raise money to buy his family. She then wanted him to work for the abolitionists, but he refused. Should Peter have done what Pickard asked? Why or why not?

2. When Peter was Nat Gist's slave, he tried to become educated. He lied to a teacher, claiming he had Gist's permission to attend school. Was Peter right in telling the teacher that his master wanted him to learn? Why or why not?

3. When Peter was trying to raise money to buy his family, some people refused to make a donation. They said it was wrong to give money to a person who owned slaves because they would then be helping to continue the practice of slavery. Write a paragraph expressing the best argument you can make challenging those who refused to give money for that reason.

4. *Seeking Additional Information.* In making decisions about such questions as those above, we often feel we need more information before we are satisfied with our judgments. Choose one of the above questions about which you would like more information than is presented in the story. What additional information would you like? Why would that information help you make a more satisfactory decision?

Freemen to the Rescue

FUGITIVE SLAVE LAW IN WISCONSIN

(State Historical Society of Wisconsin)

Glover Captured in Raid on Racine Cabin

On a cold night in March 1854, there was a rattling at the door of a small cabin near Racine, Wisconsin. Someone was trying to get in. A few black men were inside and they remained silent. The door was locked securely and the rattling stopped. One of the men was a slave who had escaped from the South. There were rumors that slave-catchers were in the area. As soon as possible the man moved on; he did not want to take a chance of being returned to slavery.

The fearful incident at the cabin was not an isolated event. There was a national debate about slavery and how runaway slaves should be treated. The arguments and emotions of the debate affected virtually everyone in the United States.

In 1850, the Congress had passed the Fugitive Slave Law. According to this law, federal commissioners in the Northern states were given the power to return escaped slaves to their masters. The escaped slaves were to have no jury trial; only the word of their supposed owners was necessary to claim the runaway. Anyone who interfered with the carrying out of the law was to be fined and placed in prison.

Northern opponents of slavery were outraged by the Fugitive Slave Law. Antislavery groups wrote resolutions condemning the law and urging its repeal. In Wisconsin, for example, one resolution said the law was "directly subversive of the principles of Liberty, in violation of Constitutional Rights, and at war with the plainest dictates of humanity."

Some people protested by working for what was known as the Underground Railroad. These people secretly helped runaway slaves by providing money, hiding them from slave-catchers, and aiding their safe arrival in Canada. Occasionally anger against the law was more open and direct. Such direct action became the case in Wisconsin.

Joshua Glover, a runaway slave, had been one of those playing cards at the cabin near Racine. He had been invited to the game by Nelson Turner, a free black man. The mysterious rattling at the door had occurred the previous evening. This night there was a loud knock at the door. "Don't open it until we know who's there," whispered Glover. Turner ignored him and immediately opened the door.

Benjamin Garland, two federal marshals, and several other men burst into the room. They rushed toward Glover and beat him to the floor. The bleeding Glover was dragged away into the cold night.

Glover had escaped from slavery in Missouri two years earlier. Garland had been his master. Now Garland, working legally under the Fugitive Slave Law, had tracked him down. Glover was taken to

Milwaukee and placed in jail. As soon as possible, Garland intended to take Glover to a federal commissioner, identify him as a runaway slave, and take him back to Missouri. Garland was following legal procedures.

It was not clear how Garland had found Glover, but people believed that Turner, the free black man, had been involved. Turner had visited Missouri the previous winter and reportedly had talked with federal officials. It was likely that Turner told them about Glover, but it was not clear why Turner would have done so. It was possible that he hoped for a reward from Garland or that he feared punishment under the Fugitive Slave Law, because he knew Glover was a runaway slave. One thing is certain—Glover was captured.

It appeared that Glover would be returned to slavery. There were some people in Wisconsin, however, who were determined to prevent such an outcome. Sherman Booth was one of them.

When Booth—a newspaper editor—heard of Glover's capture, he was furious. He had long been a loud and active antislavery advocate. He often spoke at public meetings, and his newspaper editorials practically screamed against slavery and the Fugitive Slave Law.

On Saturday, March 11, Booth mounted his horse and rode into Milwaukee. Along the way he stopped and urged people to attend a protest meeting in front of the courthouse. It was reported that he shouted "Freemen to the rescue!!"

Later in the day a few thousand people gathered near the courthouse. Speeches were given and the crowd roared its disapproval of slavery, slave-catchers, and the Fugitive Slave Law. One speaker said that the people should take the law into their own hands in protest or they might become slaves themselves. Booth gave a number of speeches. He said that the people should not break the law but should do everything possible to show their disgust with it.

Late in the day some angry members of the crowd took action. They charged the jailhouse where Glover was being held. Doors were battered down, and Glover was released and was whisked away. In a few days Glover found himself safely across the Canadian border.

Booth had not been with the mob that attacked the jail, but he was considered the one who inspired the people to take action. Booth later said that he was trying to get a trial for Glover and that he opposed the violent mob action. Nonetheless, Booth was regarded as the man who brought about Glover's escape. In his newspaper Booth boldly wrote: "We send greetings to the Free States of the Union, that, in Wisconsin, the Fugitive Slave Law is repealed! The first attempt to enforce the law, in this state, has signally, gloriously failed! NO MORE COMPROMISE WITH SLAVERY!"

Many people were pleased that Glover had been freed but did not approve of the mob violence. One newspaper editor wrote that the people hated to see law-breaking but that the laws dealing with slavery were so "inherently unjust that no good man can or will obey them."

Federal authorities took quick action. On March 15, Booth was arrested and charged with helping Glover escape. Before his trial began, Booth and his lawyer, Bryon Paine, went to the Wisconsin Supreme Court.

At the state court Paine argued that the Fugitive Slave Law was unconstitutional. He said that because no jury trial was allowed, accused runaway slaves were losing their liberty without the due process of law guaranteed by the Constitution of the United States. He also presented a states' rights argument. He said that since each state originally had agreed to the Constitution, each state could decide whether or not a federal law was constitutional. By his argument the state court had the right to decide on the constitutionality of the Fugitive Slave Law.

The court agreed with Paine's position. The judges said the law was unconstitutional and Booth should be set free. The decision was publicized widely. Antislave groups throughout the nation praised the court and lawyer Paine.

Booth and Paine's victory celebration was short-lived. Federal officials believed the state court had exceeded its legal authority by declaring a federal law unconstitutional. Booth was rearrested in the summer and held for trial in a federal court.

The jury convicted Booth of aiding in the escape of Glover. He was sentenced to one month in jail and fined $1,000. Again Booth went to the state court and, again, the court ordered him freed.

The legal controversy continued. Finally, late in 1858, the Booth case reached the Supreme Court of the United States. Things did not look promising for Booth. In the previous year the Supreme Court, under Chief Justice Roger Taney, had ruled against Dred Scott, a slave seeking his freedom. The Court had said that slaves were property like any other piece of merchandise. Because of this, Taney said, the Fifth Amendment of the Constitution applied. According to the amendment, people were not to be denied their property except under due process of law. Slaves were property and the government was to protect slaveowners' property rights. Given the Court's opinion in the Dred Scott case, it was unlikely that the judges would support Booth.

The Court ruled against Booth. It said the Fugitive Slave Law was constitutional and that the state courts of Wisconsin had no right to interfere with federal laws. Taney said that if states had the power to decide which federal laws they would obey, it would be virtually impossible to enforce any federal laws consistently throughout the states. Booth was rearrested in March 1860 and placed in jail again.

In the meantime, Booth's former lawyer, Paine, had been elected to the Wisconsin Supreme Court. Booth again appealed to the state court, but Paine ruled against him. Paine said that the Booth case was now a federal matter and that the state court could not legally take action. The judgment of the United States Supreme Court prevailed.

While Booth was in jail a number of public meetings were held and speeches were delivered praising states' rights and condemning the federal government's treatment of Booth. Another jail break was planned and, on August 1, 1860, a group of men entered the Milwaukee jail. They overpowered the jailer and helped Booth to freedom.

Booth was at large for over a month before he was recaptured by federal officers and returned to jail. Eventually Booth was freed legally. In March 1861, just before newly elected President Lincoln took office, Booth was pardoned by President Buchanan.

The major sources for this story were:

Clark, James I. *Wisconsin Defies the Fugitive Slave Law: The Case of Sherman M. Booth.* Madison, Wis.: The State Historical Society of Wisconsin, 1955.

Mason, Vroman. "The Fugitive Slave Law in Wisconsin." Bachelor of Literature thesis, University of Wisconsin—Madison, 1895.

ACTIVITIES FOR "FREEMEN TO THE RESCUE"

Answer all questions on a separate sheet of paper.

Historical Understanding

Answer briefly:

1. What were the provisions of the Fugitive Slave Law?

2. What was the Underground Railroad?

3. Briefly explain the idea of states' rights.

4. What argument did Justice Taney give in his ruling on the Dred Scott case?

Reviewing the Facts of the Case

Answer briefly:

1. Identify the following men: Garland, Glover, Turner, Booth, Paine.

2. Why did antislavery groups in the North oppose the Fugitive Slave Law?

3. Why did Garland take Glover to Milwaukee?

4. When Booth was arrested, with what crime was he charged?

5. Why did Booth and Paine first go to the Wisconsin Supreme Court? What did the state court decide?

6. What did the United States Supreme Court decide in the Booth case? What reasons were given in its decision?

Analyzing Ethical Issues

In this story there were many times that people had to make ethical decisions. In making such decisions people decide what they think is right or wrong, fair or unfair. Find four incidents in which people made ethical decisions and write a sentence describing each as illustrated in this example:

Some people thought it was right to break into jail to free Glover.

Expressing Your Reasoning

1. Acting out of hatred of the Fugitive Slave Law and the emotions stirred up by speeches in front of the courthouse, a group of people broke into jail and freed Glover. Was it right or wrong for them to do that? Why or why not?

2. Some people helped runaway slaves to escape to freedom even though they were violating the Fugitive Slave Law. Were these

people wrong in helping slaves escape? Why or why not? Does the
fact the Supreme Court said the law was constitutional affect your
judgment in any way? Why or why not? Write a paragraph expressing your position.

3. *Seeking Additional Information.* In making decisions about such
   questions as those above, we often feel we need more information
   before we are satisfied with our judgments. Choose one of the
   above questions about which you would like more information
   than is presented in the story. What additional information would
   you like? Why would that information help you make a more
   satisfactory decision?

Quoth the Raven: No! No! No!

SAM HOUSTON

(Texas State Library, Archives Division)

Sam Houston

On the afternoon of October 22, 1836, a president was inaugurated: Sam Houston, the first president of the Republic of Texas. At the age of 43, he had already lived a full life of adventure that few people could match. There was more to come.

Sam had been a restless teenager on the Tennessee frontier. He went to live with friendly Cherokee Indians. One Cherokee chieftain, Oolooteka, adopted Sam and named him the Raven.

Later, under the command of Andrew Jackson, young Sam Houston fought in the War of 1812. He was badly wounded.

After the war, with the encouragement of Jackson, Sam Houston entered Tennessee politics. He was elected to the United States Congress and later became governor of Tennessee. Some thought that he would make an excellent president of the United States.

Because of personal problems, Sam decided to leave public life. Alone, he moved westward.

In 1832 he entered Texas. Texas belonged to Mexico but many Texans sought independence and a military struggle began. Houston became commander of the Texas troops and led them to victory. Sam was a hero. He became president of the new Republic of Texas.

When Texas became independent of Mexico, there were many people in the United States and Texas who hoped the territory would become a part of the United States. Many Texans owned slaves, and if the state entered the Union it would be a slave state. Antislavery groups protested. Congressman John Quincy Adams of Massachusetts argued that proslavery forces were plotting to expand slavery. For a time, attempts to bring Texas into the Union were stalled.

Sam Houston did not oppose slavery. His family had owned slaves, and Chief Oolooteka had owned slaves. In 1840 he married Margaret Lea of Alabama, and she brought some slaves to Texas. Sam believed that Southerners had a right to own slaves and that slavery was necessary for the Southern economy. He also knew that there were strong antislavery feelings in parts of the United States, and he feared the slavery issue could rip apart the Union. Sam loved Texas, but he also loved the Union. In later years he often quoted Andrew Jackson's statement: "The Federal Union, it must be preserved."

Feelings about slavery were strong in the United States. So were feelings about expanding the size of the country. Many people believed it was natural and right that the United States should extend to the Pacific Ocean. This idea was called "manifest destiny." Feelings for expansion reached a peak with the election of James Polk as president in 1844. Polk favored national expansion. Before he was inaugurated, in March 1845, Texas was annexed to the United States.

At that time United States senators were elected by their state legislatures rather than by a direct vote of the people. The Texas legislature elected Sam Houston as one of its senators, and he went to Washington to represent his state. The Raven had never flown higher. By 1848, the United States stretched from the Atlantic to the Pacific. The Oregon Territory had been obtained through negotiations with England. Most of the rest of the area was obtained from Mexico after that nation's defeat in the Mexican War of 1846–1848. Expansionist desires had been fulfilled. Now the great question was: Shall slavery be permitted in the new territories?

Sectional differences began to show in the congressional debate about slavery in Oregon. Most Southerners wanted slavery to be permitted in the new territory. Senator John C. Calhoun of South Carolina said that slaves were property, and if Southerners wished to move to the new territory, they should be allowed to take their property. In his view Congress had no right to take away peoples' property just because they might want to settle in a new area of the country. Calhoun's arguments did not carry the day, and slavery was prohibited in the Oregon Territory. Although he was a Southerner, Sam Houston cast his vote for a slave-free Oregon.

Most Southerners were outraged at Houston's vote. He was called a traitor to his region. Sam stood his ground in spite of the protests. He said that he was a man of the South but also a man of the Union. He feared sectional differences over slavery could lead to possible war, and he wanted to avoid stirring up violent feelings. He said it was unlikely that Southerners would want to move to Oregon anyway. Also, the Missouri Compromise of 1820 had established a line north of which slavery was not to be permitted. Sam believed that agreement had helped hold the Union together and that it should be continued in dealing with slavery in the new territories.

The debate over slavery in Oregon was mild compared with what was to come. In January 1854, discussion began on the Kansas-Nebraska bill. Stephen Douglas, senator from Illinois, had introduced the bill, which said that the people living in the Kansas-Nebraska territories should have the right to decide if they wanted to permit slavery. His idea was called "popular sovereignty." Supporters of the bill said that popular sovereignty was the only truly democratic way to decide on the status of slavery in the territories.

Bitter sectional differences arose in the intense debates. Northern opponents of slavery objected to the bill because it would permit slavery in new territories, even in areas above the Old Missouri Compromise line. Southerners generally supported the bill because it would permit the extension of slavery into new territories. Southerners were also concerned that if slavery were outlawed in new territories, then new states admitted to the Union from those areas would upset the balance between slave and free states. Free states would out-number slave states and would probably vote against the slave states on national issues. A majority of free states might even try to abolish slavery in the South.

Douglas' idea appealed to some Northern senators, and it became clear that the bill would pass easily when the vote was taken. Sam Houston realized that fact. He also realized that the Texas legislature, which had elected him, strongly supported the bill. As with the Oregon bill, however, Sam feared possible disunion over the slavery question. When the time came to vote, Sam gave a speech proclaiming the need for peace and union. He voted against the bill. Nonetheless the Kansas-Nebraska Act became law.

Sam seemed to be the only Southerner standing against his region. To many Southerners he seemed to be a Benedict Arnold. One newspaper editor wrote: "Nothing can justify this treachery; nor can anything save the traitor from the deep damnation which such treason may merit." The Texas legislature voted to condemn Sam's action. Many people said he should resign, because he had failed to represent his state with his vote. Sam refused to resign.

Houston knew his vote would be unpopular in the South, but he believed his action was both wise and patriotic. He wanted to avoid violence and war. He predicted that the passage of the Kansas-Nebraska Act would bring violence. He was right. Kansas became a battleground between proslavery and antislavery forces and many people were killed. Sam also predicted that a northern antislavery political party would win the presidential election of 1860, and Southern states would secede from the Union as they had often threatened to do. If there were civil war, Sam believed the North, being stronger, would win: "I see my beloved South go down in the unequal contest, in a sea of blood and smoking ruin."

It was not difficult to predict Sam's political future. He knew that his days as a Texas senator were numbered. He had hoped that his national reputation would help him receive a presidential nomination, but it was not to be. James Buchanan won the presidency in 1856.

The following year Sam ran for governor of Texas and was defeated. Things looked bleak for the tall, aging Texan.

In time, some of the strong feelings against Sam mellowed. The man who had beaten him for governor proved unpopular, and Sam ran again for office in 1859. This time he won the election.

In his campaign for governor, Sam emphasized his belief in holding the United States together. Now that he was governor, his views would be put to the test.

The sectional hostilities that had been festering for decades came to a head in the election of 1860. The Democratic party was divided over whom to elect, and Republican Abraham Lincoln was the winner. Northern votes made Lincoln president. He received no support from Texas voters.

Sam Houston had opposed Lincoln's election, fearing it would lead to secession of the South. His prediction was correct. In December 1860, South Carolina seceded from the Union. Other states followed. Sam's hopes to preserve the Union were fading rapidly.

Most Texans wanted to secede as soon as possible, and Sam was under strong pressure to join the secession movement. His friends warned him that his life was in danger if he failed to urge secession. Dr. Ashbel Smith, one of Sam's best friends, advised him to work for secession. His wife, Margaret, was fearful for the future. If Sam's political career were ruined, his family would face hardships. She wrote to her mother: "Truly the present appearance of things is gloomy enough. . . . I cannot shut my eyes to the dangers that threaten us. I know that it is even probable that we may soon be rendered to poverty."

As governor, Houston tried as many legal maneuvers as possible to delay the calling of a secession vote, but he could not hold out forever. On February 23, 1861, the people of Texas voted 46,129 to 14,697 in favor of secession. The vote authorized a special secessionist convention that declared Texas a part of the Confederate States of America. The convention ordered all state officials to take an oath of loyalty to the Confederacy or to leave their positions. Sam was informed of the day designated for the loyalty oath.

The night before the oath taking was a time of great decision for Sam. He could not sleep, and he paced the halls of the governor's mansion until sunrise. After breakfast he walked to the capitol, where the loyalty oaths were to be taken.

A large crowd had gathered to watch the oath-taking ceremonies. The old Raven sat quietly whittling a pine stick. The chairman of the convention called Sam forward to take the oath. Sam did not rise and go forward. Three times his name was called and three times Sam did not move. His silence meant no, he would not take the oath.

Because of his refusal to take the oath, Sam was ordered out of office. The lieutenant governor, who had taken the oath, became governor. Sam and his family moved out of the governor's mansion.

Sam Houston's career was at an end. The Raven did not live to see the end of the Civil War. In July 1863 he died. Those near to him said he uttered two names at the end: Margaret and—Texas.

The major sources for this story were:

Friend, Llerena. *Sam Houston: The Great Designer.* Austin: University of Texas Press, 1954.
James, Marquis. *The Raven: A Biography of Sam Houston.* New York: Blue Ribbon Books, 1929.

ACTIVITIES FOR "QUOTH THE RAVEN: NO! NO! NO!"

Answer all questions on a separate sheet of paper.

Historical Understanding

Answer briefly:

1. What was the meaning of the idea *manifest destiny*?

2. How were United States senators elected at the time Sam Houston served in the Senate?

3. How did the United States' acquisition of new territories lead to sectional arguments about slavery?

4. What was the meaning of *popular sovereignty*?

Reviewing the Facts of the Case

Answer briefly:

1. After winning independence from Mexico, it took a number of years before Texas became a state. What caused the delay?

2. What were Sam Houston's opinions about slavery?

3. What was John C. Calhoun's argument in favor of expanding slavery into new territories?

4. Why did Sam Houston vote against the Kansas-Nebraska Act? Why were his views on the act so unpopular in the South?

5. Why did Sam Houston work against Lincoln's election?

Analyzing Ethical Issues

Difficult decisions are often a mix of factual and ethical issues. A factual issue is a question that asks what is or what might be. Factual issues are concerned with whether a statement is true or false, accurate or inaccurate. An ethical issue is a question that asks whether something is right or wrong, fair or unfair. One difficult decision that Sam Houston had to make concerned the Oregon Territory. He had to consider both factual and ethical issues.

For example:

Decision topic: *How to vote on the Oregon question.*

A factual issue involved was: *Would many Southerners wish to move to Oregon and take their slaves?*

An ethical issue involved was: *Should the government have the right to prohibit slavery in new territories?*

Find another instance in this story in which a difficult decision had to be made. Identify the topic of the decision and one factual and one ethical issue involved, as illustrated in the example above.

Expressing Your Reasoning

1. The Texas legislature, which had elected Sam as senator, voted to condemn him for his vote. Some people said that Sam should resign as senator because he failed to represent his state's wishes. Should Sam have resigned? Why or why not? There are times when an elected official's personal opinion differs from the vast majority of the people he or she represents. In general do you think elected officials should vote on the basis of their personal opinions or on the basis of how the majority of the people think? Explain the reasons for your position.

2. Should Sam Houston, as governor of Texas, have taken the loyalty oath? Why or why not?

3. Many believed that the people in new territories should have the right to decide whether or not slavery would be permitted in their territory. Write a paragraph stating your position opposing or supporting popular sovereignty, and give reasons for your position.

4. *Seeking Additional Information.* In making decisions about such questions as those above, we often feel we need more information before we are satisfied with our judgment. Choose one of the above questions about which you would like more information than is presented in the story. What additional information would you like? Why would that information help you make a more satisfactory decision?

Tears of Blood

ROBERT E. LEE

Robert E. Lee at Age 39

On a mid-April morning in 1861 a lone horseman rode slowly over the Potomac bridge that linked Virginia with Washington, D.C. In his military officer's uniform he looked majestic on horseback. He did not know that he was entering the nation's capital for the last time. Yet, beneath his appearance of calm dignity, he was inwardly tormented.

Colonel Robert E. Lee felt the dampness from the river as his horse clopped heavily upon the planks of the old bridge. He had been summoned to Washington for an interview with General Winfield Scott, general-in-chief of the U.S. Army. Lee's earliest army service had been under Scott. His affection for the old soldier was deep. As Lee approached Scott's office, he knew that the struggle raging within him was about to reach a climax. He would have to make a choice.

Events that burdened the lone horseman that April day were moving very quickly. Six days earlier Confederate guns had opened fire on the federal soldiers of Fort Sumter, near Charleston, South Carolina. Two days afterward the commander of this fort surrendered to South Carolina militia units.

A civil war had been threatening since the end of 1860. On December 20, in response to the election of Abraham Lincoln as president, South Carolina had seceded from the Union. The states of Mississippi, Florida, Alabama, Georgia, and Louisiana soon followed South Carolina's lead and withdrew from the Union. A Texas convention overrode that state's governor, Sam Houston, and joined the other states that had seceded.

Early in 1861 delegates from six of the seceding states met and drafted a constitution for the Confederate States of America. The Confederate Constitution resembled the Constitution of the United States. There were two major differences, however. The Confederate Constitution stressed the "sovereignty and independent character of each state." It also guaranteed the right to own slaves.

In response to the bombardment of Fort Sumter, President Lincoln had asked Congress for 75,000 troops. War between the states had come. Would Virginia, largest of the southern states, join the Confederacy? A Virginia convention was debating this issue at the moment that Colonel Lee rode into Washington.

The future of his home state weighed heavily on Colonel Lee. As he approached General Scott's office in the War Department building, he wondered what he would do if Virginia seceded. Entering the building, he drew some comfort from the fact that General Scott was a fellow Virginian.

Scene 1 of the play by John Drinkwater, entitled *Robert E. Lee*, presents a dramatic account of the meeting between these two soldiers. The characters in this part of the play are:

> The Officer (Perrin): A major of the general's staff
> The Orderly: A soldier attached to the general's staff
> Scott: Winfield Scott, general-in-chief, U.S. Army
> Lee: Robert E. Lee, Lieutenant-Colonel, U.S. Army

THE OFFICER (*indicating paper*): The recruiting reports are good this morning, sir. Over half the President's seventy-five thousand in three days.

SCOTT (*consulting the papers on his table*): Yes—yes. What's the time?

THE OFFICER: Just on twelve o'clock, sir.

SCOTT: If Virginia goes, we shall lose Lee.

THE OFFICER: Surely not, sir. A soldier all his life.

SCOTT: I hope not, but I think so.
   (*The Orderly comes in.*)

THE ORDERLY: Colonel Lee is here, sir.

SCOTT: Ask him to come in.
   (*The Orderly goes.*)

SCOTT: You needn't go, Perrin. Take notes.

PERRIN: Yes, sir.
   (*The Orderly shows in ROBERT E. LEE, at this time a Lieutenant-Colonel in the U.S. Army. The Orderly goes.*)

SCOTT: Good-Morning, Colonel.

LEE: Good-morning, sir.

SCOTT: This is Major Perrin. You've no objection to his hearing what we have to say?

LEE: No, certainly.

SCOTT: Sit down, please. (*They sit.*)

SCOTT: It is at the President's suggestion that I asked you to come.

LEE: I am honoured, sir.

SCOTT: The problem is at the moment common—lamentably common. But we felt that your case was a special one, or rather, in a special sense a representative one. The esteem in which you stand in Virginia, and your personal record in the

army, make your views of particular—as I say of representative
—importance. We considered that a personal interview was
the proper way of learning them.

LEE: I welcome your confidence.

SCOTT: You are aware that six states have already declared for
secession from the Union?

LEE: I understood five.

SCOTT: Alabama's decision comes this morning.

LEE: I had not heard.

SCOTT: Do you approve?

LEE: If I were a mere spectator of events, I should say no.

SCOTT: A spectator?

LEE: It can hardly be an abstract question with me, you see, sir.

SCOTT: You mean Virginia?

LEE: Being a Virginian, yes, sir.

SCOTT: Your state, you mean, right or wrong?

LEE: Right and wrong are such dangerous words for men to use,
ever.

SCOTT: Duty is a plain thing, Colonel Lee.

LEE: It should be sir. But for it we may have to forfeit the good
opinion of men that we cherish. My duty may not seem to
me, for example, what you consider it should mean.

SCOTT: Your mind is fixed?

LEE: No—it is very gravely troubled.

SCOTT: Virginia's decision is not yet announced.

LEE: The Convention was sitting late into the night, I hear.

SCOTT: I gather that the indications are that she will follow the
others.

LEE: In view of what has happened, I fear so.

SCOTT: You fear so?

LEE: Yes. I am opposed to secession on principle. More, I do not
think the issue upon which it is proposed is a sufficient one. I
would gladly see every slave freed rather than that the Union
should be broken.

SCOTT: You hold your commission under that Union.

LEE: I know sir. It has made my life a fortunate one.

SCOTT: Then where can be the difference in opinion of which you speak?

LEE: I am two things, sir. I am not a statesman, nor do I in any other way control public policy. I am a soldier. But before that I am a citizen of Virginia. If my state decides to dispute the authority of the service in which I have for so long had the honour to be, I may regret the decision, but I may feel it my duty to respect it in my action.

SCOTT: Then let me put it more explicitly. The Government, as you know, has declared war on the rebel states.

LEE: The seceding states.

SCOTT: The rebel states, Colonel Lee. Be plain about that. Major Anderson has been forced to surrender at Fort Sumter. The President's appeal for seventy-five thousand men is being answered eagerly. We are facing no holiday campaign. Other states will doubtless join the rebels. Two years will hardly see it through.

LEE: I should have said four, sir.

SCOTT: I was discussing the situation as a whole with President Lincoln yesterday evening. You were much spoken of. There is no officer in the army of whom he has a higher opinion, and I was privileged to say how just I considered that opinion to be. He instructed me to offer you the command of all Union forces in the field. I may say for myself that I think that even so great a distinction has been fully earned, Colonel Lee, and I could make the offer to no one with so much satisfaction.

LEE: The President's confidence, and yours, sir, are very much above my merit. I cannot express my sense of this. But what am I to say?

SCOTT: To say? How do you mean, to say?

LEE: Virginia has not spoken.

SCOTT: The army that you serve calls you to lead it. And you ask what you shall say.

LEE: To lead it against whom?

SCOTT: Against rebels to their country.

LEE: It may be against Virginia.

SCOTT: Then still against rebels.

LEE: Against my own people.

SCOTT: You are a soldier, you say. You are under orders.

LEE: I have been allowed to serve under you, sir. I know what discipline is—I do not need to be reminded. There have been times when I have obeyed orders with no very light heart . . . Now obedience may be against my public loyalty to the soil that made me. My Virginia. You may be asking me to invade, perhaps to destroy my own homeland. Do you wonder that I answer "What am I to say"?

Who was this lieutenant-colonel being offered command of the entire Union Army at such a critical hour? How did this Virginia soldier come to face such an agonizing decision? The answers to these questions can be traced to the early years of the American republic.

Robert E. Lee was no ordinary Virginian. Like Washington and Jefferson he was one of that state's most brightly shining stars. In 1799 John Adams wrote to a friend that the Lee family had "more merit in it than any other family." Two Lees had stood with Adams at the signing of the Declaration of Independence.

Robert was born in 1807 when his father, Light-Horse Harry Lee, was 51 years old. Of Robert's father it was said that he had "come out of his mother's womb a soldier." Light-Horse Harry was a military hero of the Revolutionary War. He played a major role in bringing Cornwallis to defeat at Yorktown. Congress had voted him a medal. After the war, Light-Horse Harry Lee served three terms as governor of Virginia.

In his later years, Light-Horse Harry followed a path to ruin. His failed land speculation schemes wrecked his family financially. In 1811 he became involved in a violent fight. The beating he took left him crippled and disfigured. He never regained his health. When Robert was 11 years old, his father died a broken man.

With his father dead, and his two older brothers away, Robert ran the family's modest brick house in Alexandria. He served as housekeeper, supervised the marketing, and managed the garden and stable. He was devoted to his sickly mother.

Robert decided to follow in his father's military footsteps. He secured an appointment to West Point, the U.S. military academy. There he was a model cadet. He received no demerits and graduated second in his class.

Following graduation, at age 21, Robert began courting Mary Custis. Mary was beautiful, quiet, and religious. She was also the granddaughter of George Washington. Mary's father, George Washington Custis, was the adopted son of the first president. George Washington Custis had built an estate called Arlington, high in the hills above Alexandria.

Robert and Mary were married in 1830. Years later, after the death of his father-in-law, Robert became head of the Arlington estate. Robert, Mary, and their children lived comfortably there. Robert always loved the Arlington mansion that had become a national shrine to the Father of the Country. Many of the first president's belongings were kept there.

Army life deprived Robert of spending much time at home. During the Mexican War (1846–1848) he was gone for 22 months. It was in Mexico at this time that the son of Light-Horse Harry Lee made his mark as a soldier.

Lee's ability as a military engineer contributed to major U.S. victories during the war. His competence, tact, grace, and quiet manner won the favor of his superiors. During the war Lee was promoted rapidly to captain, then major, and then brevet lieutenant-colonel. He served on the staff of the commanding general and hero of the Mexican War, Winfield Scott. Scott said that his success in Mexico "was largely due to the skill, valor, and undaunted energy of Robert E. Lee." Lee had no real taste for war, however. In Mexico he was homesick for Mary, the children, and Arlington.

After the war Lee had several assignments, often supervising construction of military forts. Then, in 1852, he began three of the most pleasant years of his life. He was appointed superintendent of West Point. His family settled happily in the superintendent's house. Lee tightened discipline and raised academic standards at the military academy.

One morning Lee was informed that five cadets had liquor in their possession when they returned. The young men had been caught red-handed. Among the offenders was Fitz Lee, Robert's nephew and son of his beloved brother. Superintendent Lee ordered a court-martial trial. Fitz Lee and his comrades received stiff punishments.

Following his years at West Point, Lee was transferred to the Texas frontier. He was pleased with his new rank of lieutenant-colonel, but camp life on the frontier was lonely. Chasing Mexican bandits and Comanche Indians was a poor substitute for West Point or Arlington.

In 1859 Lee was granted a leave of absence from duty in Texas. He headed home to Arlington. While he was shopping in Alexandria one morning, a young lieutenant handed him a message. It said there had been a disturbance at Harpers Ferry. Virginia marines were being sent to the scene of the trouble. Lee was ordered to command them.

A man named John Brown had led a band of followers in seizing the federal armory at Harpers Ferry. Brown had fought against slavery in Kansas. He intended to free the slaves of Virginia and then of the whole South through armed rebellion.

When Lee arrived at Harpers Ferry, he learned that Brown and about twenty of his followers had been driven by Virginia militia into a stone fire engine house. Brown's followers had earlier shot and killed two men. Several hostages had been taken into the engine house by the insurgents.

Colonel Lee sent a message to those in the engine house demanding surrender. Those who surrendered, he promised, would be turned over to civilian authorities. The message warned that the armory was surrounded and that escape was impossible.

An officer carried the message under a white flag to the engine house. As he approached, the front door was opened a crack. Through the crack the face of a guant and grimy old man appeared. It was John Brown holding a carbine.

Brown wanted to make a deal. He asked to be allowed to pass through the army lines with his followers until they reached Maryland. There the hostages would be released. Some of the hostages called out urging the militia not to use force on Brown. "He will kill us," one shouted.

Lee would strike no bargain. He gave the signal for the marines to storm the engine house. Carbines crackled inside and smoke drifted outside. Two marines were shot, one mortally. Two of Brown's followers were killed by bayonet thrusts. Brown was taken prisoner, tried for treason and murder, convicted, and hanged. Many Northern opponents of slavery considered John Brown a hero and a martyr. In Lee's opinion Brown was a fanatic who had incited rioters to insurrection.

Although he opposed slavery, Lee did not approve of John Brown's methods for challenging it. Lee had called slavery "a moral and political evil." Once he had said: "If I owned four million slaves, I would cheerfully sacrifice them for preservation of the Union." But Lee's attitude was one of gradualism. Slavery, he believed, would best be ended by allowing it to fade gradually away. Christian charity and not force, he thought, would convince people to free the slaves.

After Harpers Ferry, in 1860, Lee was again assigned to Texas. The spirit of secession was then spreading through the South. Lee was upset to find that it had crept into the army command. He strongly disapproved of states' breaking away from the Union. In a letter to his son, Lee wrote: "It [the Constitution] was intended for 'perpetual union' so expressed in the preamble, and for establishment of a government, not a compact, which can only be dissolved by revolution, or the consent of all of the people in convention assembled."

Since the Mexican War, promotions had not come quickly to Lee. He felt resentment when he was passed over because of favoritism. He began to think his military career had stagnated. A growing sense of failure started to grip him. Adding to his gloom was the lack of enough money to maintain the Arlington estate. His salary as a lieutenant-colonel was not high enough to meet expenses. Compounding his burden was news that his wife, Mary, was becoming crippled with arthritis. Lee longed to return home to Virginia. The opportunity came with the unexpected order to report to Washington, D.C., where he was to have an interview with General Scott.

The night following the interview was a restless one for Lee. In the morning he returned home across the Potomac to Arlington. Along the way he stopped at John Mosby's drugstore in Alexandria. There he glanced at the newspaper. The headline—"VIRGINIA SECEDES"—struck him like a whip.

War would mean that Arlington, because it was so close to the capital, would soon be occupied by federal troops. The mansion would be seized and perhaps destroyed. Lee could postpone a firm response to General Scott no longer.

Alone in his bedroom Lee agonized through the night over his reply to Scott. The next morning he submitted his letter of resignation. In a letter written later that morning to his sister in Baltimore he said:

> I had to meet the question whether I should take part against my native state. With all my devotion to the Union and the feeling of loyalty and duty as an American citizen, I have not been able to make up my mind to raise my hand against my relatives, my children, my home.

Over his decision to resign from the U.S. Army, Lee's wife, Mary, remarked: "My husband has wept tears of blood."

The major sources for this story were:

Dowdey, Clifford. *Lee*. Boston: Little Brown, 1965.

Drinkwater, John. *Robert E. Lee*. Boston: Houghton Mifflin, 1923 (play excerpt from pp. 10–14).

Harwell, Richard. *Lee* (an abridgment in one volume of the four-volume *R. E. Lee* by Douglas Southall Freeman). New York: Charles Scribner's Sons, 1961.

Miers, Earl S. *Robert E. Lee, A Great Life in Brief*. New York: Alfred A. Knopf, 1956.

ACTIVITIES FOR "TEARS OF BLOOD"

Answer all questions on a separate sheet of paper.

Historical Understanding

Answer briefly:

1. What did South Carolina do in response to the election of Abraham Lincoln in 1860?

2. How was the Constitution of the Confederate States of America different from the United States Constitution?

3. Prior to the Civil War, what important contributions did members of the Lee family of Virginia make to their country?

4. What was John Brown's goal at Harpers Ferry?

5. What happened at Fort Sumter in the spring of 1861?

Reviewing the Facts of the Case

Answer briefly:

1. As a result of his marriage, what was Lee's relationship to George Washington?

2. What effects did the Mexican War have on the military career of Robert E. Lee?

3. How did Superintendent Lee respond to his nephew's breaking of the rules at West Point?

4. How did Colonel Lee handle the capture of John Brown at Harpers Ferry?

5. What was Lee's view of slavery?

6. What was Lee's position on states' secession from the Union?

7. What offer did General Scott make to Lee in the name of President Lincoln?

Analyzing Ethical Issues

In ethical matters it is important to consider the value of consistency. Ethical consistency refers to the relationship between our beliefs about what is right and our actions. To be consistent we must do what we believe we ought to do. It is often a problem for people to decide whether or not to be ethically consistent. For example, suppose someone believes it is wrong to cut in front of others waiting in line. When that person finds a long line at the movies, a friend offers a place near the front of the line. Deciding what to do may be difficult.

Consider whether or not Robert E. Lee was ethically consistent. For each of his four beliefs presented below write a sentence describing an action he took pertaining to that belief, and then decide whether the action was consistent or inconsistent with his belief. Be prepared to explain how you reached your conclusions.

For example:

BELIEF	ACTION	CONSISTENT OR INCONSISTENT
Cadets at West Point who break the rules should be punished.	*Lee recommended court-martial for his nephew, Fitz.*	*Consistent.*

1. Slavery is a moral and political evil.

2. Citizens should be loyal to their country.

3. The federal Union should be preserved.

4. One ought to help provide care for sick family members.

Expressing Your Reasoning

1. Did Robert E. Lee do the right thing when he resigned from the U.S. Army? State the reasons for your position.

2. When considering what is right, it can be helpful to evaluate the reasons given for various positions. For each of the two positions presented below, explain which reason you think is best and which you think is worst.

a. Lee should have resigned, because:
   1) a person should not take up arms against his neighbors and relatives.
   2) a Virginia convention had voted to secede and citizens of the state should obey the laws of the state.
   3) Lee had not been promoted for a long time. He was being offered a promotion by the army now only because they needed him. By resigning he could get even with the army for passing him over earlier.
   4) the federal government was violating states' rights by forcing them to remain in the Union. A soldier has no obligation to fight in a war to preserve a union that some states want to leave.
   5) his wife, Mary, was becoming crippled with arthritis and she needed his personal attention at home.
b. Lee should not have resigned, because:
   1) he took an oath of allegiance to the United States when he became a military officer. According to that oath he was obligated to obey orders.
   2) he believed that he could best protect his home and property at the Arlington estate if he stayed on as commander of the Union forces.
   3) slavery was unjust, and a Union victory would be a step toward abolition.
   4) he could help shorten the war and save lives by commanding the Union forces.
   5) Lee ought to honor the memory of George Washington. By marriage he inherited a family responsibility to uphold the tradition begun by the Father of the Country.

3. Should Colonel Lee have negotiated with John Brown over release of the hostages taken at Harpers Ferry? Why or why not?

4. Lee strictly disciplined his nephew, Fitz, when the cadet broke the rules at West Point. Some say the superintendent should have gone easier on Fitz, because the boy was his brother's son. Furthermore, it is said, Lee should not have recommended a court-martial for Fitz, because it might harm the family reputation—already damaged by the failures of Light-Horse Harry Lee. Do you agree or disagree with this argument? In a paragraph explain why.

5. *Seeking Additional Information.* In making decisions about such questions as those above, we often feel we need more information before we are satisfied with our judgments. Choose one of the above questions about which you would like more information than is presented in the story. What additional information would you like? Why would that information help you make a more satisfactory decision?

The Miseries of Dr. Mudd

DR. SAMUEL MUDD

(*Courtesy of Dr. Richard D. Mudd*)

Dr. Samuel Mudd

Tired and weary, Dr. Samuel Mudd went to bed one Friday night in 1865. Life was not easy on his farm in swampy southern Maryland. The Civil War had made life difficult in many ways.

Dr. Mudd had not wanted the nation to separate, but he did want slavery to continue. He did not have many patients in the area, and he needed the few slaves he had to work the tobacco fields, to provide an income for his family. When slavery was outlawed in Maryland, farmers had to hire workers. Sam could not afford to hire many workers and his profits suffered. Now he was spending long hours in the fields. It seemed that going to bed bone-tired was becoming a way of life.

Southern Maryland was on the border between the North and the South during the war. Across the Potomac River was the state of Virginia, with its city of Richmond the capital of the Confederacy. Maryland had voted to stay in the Union, but many Northern leaders suspected southern Marylanders of disloyalty. It was true that many people in that area were sympathetic to the South.

Early in the war, President Lincoln agreed with some of his advisors that any Marylander suspected of disloyalty should be arrested by the military. Thousands of troops poured into southern Maryland and many people were imprisoned without trials or significant evidence against them.

Dr. Mudd was careful about what he did and said, and he was never arrested. His wife Frances' brother, Jeremiah Dyer, was suspected of disloyalty, and he asked Sam for help. Sam allowed Jeremiah to hide out in some bushes on the farm and supplied him with food and blankets. The soldiers searching for Jeremiah Dyer were unsuccessful and eventually left the area.

At four o'clock in the morning on Saturday, April 15, 1865, there was a loud knocking at Sam's door. At the door was a scruffy young man who had been riding hard. A few yards away in the dim light Sam could see another man sitting on a horse. The young man spoke anxiously. He and his friend were riding to Washington and his friend's horse had fallen and broken the man's leg. Someone in the area had directed them to Dr. Mudd.

The man with the broken leg had his head wrapped in a shawl. He also wore a beard and a moustache. In the house, Sam cut the riding boot from the man's swollen leg and put a splint on the broken area. Then he helped the man to an upstairs bedroom and urged him to rest.

Later in the day, Sam and the younger man rode to nearby Bryan-town to see if they could get a carriage for the injured man. As they approached town, soldiers were seen riding about. For some reason, the young man decided to return to Sam's house. Sam rode on into town.

There was excitement and confusion in town. Sam soon found out why. The previous night, April 14, Abraham Lincoln had been shot in the head while attending a play at Ford's Theater in Washington. The assassin, an actor named Booth, had escaped and was fleeing south-ward. His escape route led through southern Maryland. It was believed another man was riding with him.

Mudd rode slowly home. He had voted for Lincoln in the election of 1864, because Lincoln had said that he would treat the defeated South fairly. Now he was dead, and there was no telling what would happen. Sam stopped at a neighbor's house and told him of the tragedy; he did not mention the two strangers at his house.

When he reached home, he found the two strangers waiting by their horses. They asked for some directions and rode off. Although they had said they were going to Washington, they did not ride in that direction.

After Sam told Frances of the assassination, they discussed the two strangers. Before he left, the injured man had shaved off his mous-tache. As he left, Frances noticed that he was wearing a false beard. Why was he trying to disguise himself? The question must have entered their minds: Was the injured stranger John Wilkes Booth, the man who shot Lincoln? In fact he was.

Sam wondered if he should report the strangers to the soldiers in town. Frances asked him not to do it until the following day. It was getting late and she did not want to stay alone at night during such dangerous times. Sam remained at home.

The next day, after Easter church services, Sam told his cousin about the strangers. Sam asked his cousin to inform the troops about the visit. The following day the soldiers were informed and on Tuesday detectives came to Sam's house.

Sam told his story. The name Booth was never mentioned by anyone, but Sam said it seemed suspicious that the injured man would shave his moustache. The detectives returned to town. They reported that Dr. Mudd seemed to be withholding information.

In the meantime, Booth and his companion Herold found shelter. Colonel Cox, a strong supporter of the South, allowed them to hide on his land. Cox asked Thomas Jones to help Booth and Herold escape to Virginia. Jones had heard of the big reward but, on seeing the exhausted, injured Booth he felt sorry for him. Jones got a boat and the fugitives were able to escape to Virginia.

At the same time Booth and Herold were escaping, the detectives returned to Dr. Mudd. Sam produced the boot he had cut from the injured man. Inside was written, "John Wilkes." Sam was asked what he knew about Booth. Sam said he had not recognized the injured man as Booth but that he had met John Wilkes Booth in the past. Booth had been in the area the previous November looking to buy land as an investment. Sam had shown him around the area and invited him for dinner. In writing, Dr. Mudd claimed that was the only time he had met Mr. Booth. It was later discovered he was not telling the whole truth.

Although Booth claimed to be looking for land, he was actually scouting for an escape route from Washington. Booth had planned to kidnap President Lincoln and rush him to the South. Lincoln would be held for ransom. There were thousands of Confederate troops in Northern prisons. Lincoln would be traded for them and they could return to fight for the South. The war ended before Booth could carry out his plot.

Booth then sought revenge for the defeated South. Along with others, he planned to kill Lincoln, Secretary of State Seward, Vice-President Johnson, and war hero Uylsses Grant. Only Lincoln actually died. Booth's partners made many errors and the others lived.

The detectives interviewing Mudd did not know all these details, but they were suspicious of Mudd. Sam was taken to Washington and placed in prison to await trial.

Booth and Herold thought they would be treated as heroes in Virginia, but they were wrong. Booth's leg had become infected and he went to the home of a Dr. Stewart. Stewart turned him away and refused to treat the leg.

A farmer named Garrett allowed Booth and Herold to stay in his barn. Federal troops had picked up their trail and soon tracked them to the barn. The troops were ordered to capture Booth alive. They surrounded the barn and set it afire to drive him out. Herold quickly surrendered. Booth seemed determined to stay in the barn. Corporal Boston Corbett, later saying that God had directed him, put his gun through a crack in the barn and shot Booth. He was pulled from the barn and died a few hours later.

The great manhunt was over. Booth was dead. Attention was now focused on the trial of those who may have helped him. In addition to Mudd and Herold, there were six others to be tried. The prisoners were guarded closely and treated poorly. Much of the time they had to wear tight canvas hoods with padding over their eyes and ears. Small holes permitted them to breathe and eat.

Secretary of War Edwin Stanton had been directing the investigation. He was determined that the defendants be tried quickly in a military court. Civilian courts were too slow, he thought, and defendants might have more rights there. Some of Stanton's advisors disagreed with him. They said that none of the defendants was in the military, the war was over, and civilian courts were operating. Nonetheless, Stanton was convinced they were all guilty and a military court could move quickly. Also, the public was outraged by the assassination and wanted swift punishment for the guilty.

The military trial began in May 1865. All the prisoners were charged with the same crime: working with Booth to kill Lincoln and the others. Dr. Mudd was stunned when he heard the charges against him.

The prisoners were required to wear chains during the trial; all except Mary Surratt. Because she was a woman, the court decided she should not have to wear them. Each defendant had a lawyer, but the court would not allow the defendants to speak. They could only listen to the discussions and the testimony of witnesses.

A number of lawyers refused to defend the prisoners. Most likely they felt their reputations would suffer if they got involved. Eventually, however, lawyers were chosen. Sam was fortunate in having a good lawyer who was able to show that many of the witnesses against him were either lying or confused. Nonetheless, things did not look good for Dr. Mudd. It turned out that he had met Booth for a brief time in Washington the previous December. Mudd claimed to have only met Booth once before in Maryland. There was no evidence that Mudd had any knowledge of Booth's plans, but suspicion ruled the day. He was judged guilty along with all the others.

Mary Surratt, David Herold, and two of the others were sentenced to death. The rest received prison sentences. Dr. Mudd was sentenced to life imprisonment at hard labor. The military judges had voted five to four that Mudd should hang but six votes were necessary for the death penalty.

One of the judges, General Lew Wallace, best known today as the author of *Ben Hur*, apparently believed that Sam was innocent. He is reported to have said, however, "The deed is done. . . . Somebody must suffer for it, and he may as well suffer as anybody else."

Sam was shocked and bitter about the verdict. He later said: "Before a word of evidence was heard, my case was prejudiced and I was already condemned on the strength of wild rumor and misrepresentation. . . . I felt ashamed of my species and lost faith forever in mankind."

On Friday, July 7, 1865, the four condemned prisoners were hanged. There had been appeals to spare Mary Surratt from the rope; many thought it was wrong to hang a woman. The appeals failed and she died with the others.

Frances Mudd and her lawyers were determined to get Sam freed. He had been sentenced to a penitentiary in Albany, New York. Perhaps they could get the courts there to reopen the case. In calmer times, in a civilian court, they believed Dr. Mudd's innocence could be shown. They would not get their chance. Secretary of War Stanton transferred Mudd to a military prison, Fort Jefferson. It was located on the Dry Tortugas, islands west of southern Florida.

The islands were hot, smelly, and insect-ridden. Fort Jefferson was reputed to be one of the worst prisons anywhere. Life for the prisoners was horrid; many called it a living death. Even the soldiers who served as guards despised the place. To prevent mutiny, the soldiers were only required to serve there for a few months before being replaced. When Dr. Mudd entered the prison, he saw a sign above the gate: "All Hope Abandon, Ye Who Enter Here."

It would have been easy to abandon all hope. For long periods of time Sam was not allowed to receive any mail. When mail was permitted, it was censored by the authorities. When packages arrived, guards opened them and took what items pleased them. Prisoners were also subject to cruel punishments.

Frances worked constantly for Sam's release. She urged President Johnson to pardon him. Johnson believed that Sam should be released, but he had problems of his own. Members of Congress, the Radical Republicans, believed that Johnson was too soft on the South and wanted to impeach him. If he pardoned a person convicted of playing a part in Lincoln's assassination, it would make him look pro-Southern. He sympathized with Mrs. Mudd but said he could do nothing at that time.

Prisoners occasionally escaped from the fort, but Mudd felt an escape attempt would make him look guilty of working with Booth. His despair increased. In one letter to Frances he wrote: "I am often cast down by depressing thoughts about you and all near and dear to me. . . . The thought often arises, or the question is asked within myself, 'Shall I ever see home again, or those fond ones left behind?'"

In September 1865, Dr. Mudd had a chance to escape. A supply ship had come to the fort. A young seaman named Henry Kelly agreed to help Dr. Mudd and slipped him on board. Sam hid beneath some planks waiting anxiously for the ship to set sail. Unfortunately for him, his absence was discovered, and soldiers pulled him from the ship.

The commander of the fort knew that someone must have helped Sam in his attempted escape. He threatened Sam with severe punishment unless he revealed who helped him. Dr. Mudd gave in and identified Kelly as the man who helped him. Both men were placed in the dungeon.

The horrors of prison life continued. One prisoner described the food: "Coffee was brought to our quarters in a dirty, greasy bucket, always with grease swimming upon its surface: bread, rotten fish, and meal all mixed together, the one spoiling the other by contact." Early in 1866, Sam described his condition: "Imagine one loaded down with heavy chains, locked up in a wet, damp room, twelve hours out of every twenty-four during working days, and all day on Sundays and holidays. No exercise allowed except in the limited space of a small room, and with irons on. . . . My legs and ankles are swollen and sore, pains in my shoulder and back are frequent. My hair began falling out some time ago."

Torture of the prisoners was common. One punishment was being hanged by the thumbs for hours. Another was to carry a heavy cannon ball around in circles in the hot sun. Occasionally a prisoner was beaten to death. In the autumn of 1867, more death was to come; not by the stab of a soldier's bayonet, however, but from the sting of a mosquito's tiny needle.

One of the most dreaded diseases of the time was yellow fever. Epidemics killing hundreds of people were common. Years later, medical research would discover that a mosquito bite spread the disease. In Dr. Mudd's time no one knew.

A yellow fever epidemic started slowly at Fort Jefferson. Soon it gathered momentum. Officers and guards seemed most susceptible and every day more of them came down with the disease. The island was quarantined—no one was allowed to leave or enter.

In early September, the fort's doctor caught the disease and died. Then there was no doctor to treat the stricken men. Dr. Mudd thought hard about what was happening. He had some experience in treating yellow fever and wondered if he should offer his services. He remembered the military trial, the lies of witnesses, his banishment to Fort Jefferson, and the tortures inflicted on the prisoners. Why should he help anyone? Also, he thought, what if his patients died? Would he be accused of poisoning them for revenge? Some fellow prisoners urged him to remain silent, but Dr. Mudd decided differently. He offered his help, and Major Stone, commander of the fort, happily accepted.

Sam worked constantly, bringing relief where he could. The epidemic raged. Many of the sickest patients had coffins placed next to their cots, so they could be removed quickly when they died. Another doctor was sent to the island, and he and Dr. Mudd worked around the clock trying to save patients. Almost 300 of the 400 people on the island contracted the disease. Major Stone left the island but died of the fever while on ship. The two doctors were, in effect, now in command of the fort.

At this time it would have been quite easy for Sam to escape. He considered the idea but decided to remain and treat the sick. By the time the epidemic ended, about forty of the afflicted had died. The survivors credited the doctors' courageous work in saving them. All of the soldiers signed a petition recommending that Sam be pardoned. Apparently, President Johnson never received the petition, and nothing came of it.

In December 1867, Mudd was visited by William Gleason. Gleason was working with the Radical Republicans who hoped to impeach Johnson. As part of their plans they wanted to show that President Johnson had been involved in the plans to kill Lincoln! It appears that Gleason wanted Mudd to sign a document that would make it appear that Johnson was involved. If Sam failed to sign, he was threatened with punishment. If he did sign, there was a good chance he would be set free. Dr. Mudd refused to sign any untruthful statement, and Mr. Gleason left without getting what he wanted.

President Johnson was not convicted on the impeachment charges and, at the end of his term in office, he signed a pardon for Dr. Mudd.

The constant efforts of his wife and friends finally succeeded. Sam was freed.

Dr. Mudd returned to his family and his farm. Although still in his early thirties, he looked years older. In January 1883, at the age of 49, Dr. Samuel Mudd died. Decades later, President Eisenhower ordered that a plaque praising Dr. Mudd for his fight against yellow fever be placed in Fort Jefferson.

The major sources for this story were:

Carter, Samuel, III. *The Riddle of Dr. Mudd*. New York: G. P. Putnam's Sons, 1974.
Higdon, Hal. *The Union vs. Dr. Mudd*. Chicago: Follett, 1964.
Roscoe, Theodore. *The Web of Conspiracy: The Complete Story of the Men Who Murdered Abraham Lincoln*. Englewood Cliffs, N.J.: Prentice-Hall, 1959.

ACTIVITIES FOR "THE MISERIES OF DR. MUDD"

Answer all questions on a separate sheet of paper.

Historical Understanding

Answer briefly:

1. Identify two ways that the Civil War made life difficult for Dr. Mudd and others in southern Maryland.

2. For what purposes did John Wilkes Booth want to kidnap President Lincoln?

3. Why did the Radical Republicans want to impeach Andrew Johnson?

Reviewing the Facts of the Case

Answer briefly:

1. Why did Jeremiah Dyer seek help from Dr. Mudd?

2. How many times had Dr. Mudd met Mr. Booth before the assassination? How did this affect him at the trial?

3. When and how did Dr. Mudd report the strangers who visited him?

4. Why did Secretary Stanton want a military trial?

5. What were some ways that life at Fort Jefferson was dreadful?

6. What did Dr. Mudd do when the epidemic hit the fort?

7. Why did President Johnson delay pardoning Dr. Mudd?

Analyzing Ethical Issues

There is agreement on the answer to some questions. For other questions there is disagreement about the answer. We call these questions issues. Issues can be categorized as factual or ethical. A factual issue asks whether something is true or false, accurate or inaccurate. An ethical issue asks whether something is right or wrong, fair or unfair. Factual issues ask what *is;* ethical issues ask what *ought to be.*

For example:

Was Dr. Mudd involved in the plot to kill Lincoln?   *Factual.*

Should Sam have immediately reported the strangers' visit? *Ethical.*

For each of the following questions, decide whether the issue is factual or ethical, as illustrated in the example above.

1. Did Dr. Mudd withhold information from the authorities?

2. Did Dr. Mudd have an obligation to treat Mr. Booth's injured leg?

3. Should Mary Surratt have been treated differently from the other defendants?

4. Would Dr. Mudd have been found innocent if he had been tried in a civilian court?

5. Was it wrong for Sam Mudd to report Henry Kelly?

6. Would most of the men on the island have died if Sam had not worked so hard to save them?

7. Should Andrew Johnson have pardoned Sam Mudd when Frances first asked him to?

There are many other factual and ethical issues suggested in the story. Write a sentence identifying one of each type of issue.

Expressing Your Reasoning

1. In spite of the misfortunes that had beset him, Dr. Mudd volunteered his services when the yellow fever epidemic hit Fort Jefferson. Many of his patients were soldiers who had mistreated him and the other prisoners. Should Dr. Mudd have volunteered to help? Why or why not?

2. Sam was caught attempting to escape from the prison. When threatened by the officers, he revealed the name of the man who helped him. Should he have done that? Why or why not?

3. Sam allowed his brother-in-law to hide out on his farm. Should he have done that? Why or why not? Write a paragraph expressing your opinion.

4. *Seeking Additional Information.* In making decisions about such questions as those above, we often feel we need more information before we are satisfied with our judgments. Choose one of the above questions about which you would like more information than is presented in the story. What additional information would you like? Why would it help you make a more satisfactory decision?

Pioneer Suffragist

SUSAN B. ANTHONY

Susan B. Anthony

The importance of Kansas in the great affairs of the nation began in 1854. That year, the Kansas-Nebraska Act created two new territories in the west: Kansas and Nebraska. Slaves had not been allowed in that area since 1820. The two new territories were north of the Missouri Compromise line drawn earlier by Congress to separate free soil from slaveholding areas.

The Kansas-Nebraska Act abolished the old dividing line. Under the new law, Kansas and Nebraska could each choose whether or not to permit slavery. This new choice was called popular sovereignty. It plunged the nation into a violent controversy. Most Southern Democrats welcomed an opportunity to extend slavery. Most Northern Republicans protested against opening the new territories to slavery.

As a battleground over slavery, Kansas foreshadowed the conflict soon to engulf the nation. Northern and Southern settlers began a race to take control of the new territory. Antislavery settlers moved in and founded Lawrence, Topeka, and other settlements. Proslavery settlers from Missouri moved over the border into other Kansas towns including Atchison, Leavenworth, and Lecompton. Violence erupted in what became known as Bleeding Kansas. Federal troops were sent in to restore order. Those opposed to slavery finally prevailed. In 1861, on the eve of the Civil War, Kansas was admitted to the Union as a free state.

The battles of the 1850s to keep slaves out of Kansas had brought a large number of *abolitionists* (those who wanted to end slavery) to settle in the territory. Many of them became Republicans. During Reconstruction, which followed the Civil War, they hoped to win political rights for the *freedmen* (former male slaves). *Suffrage* (the right to vote) was considered most important. Some Kansas Republicans believed that the right to vote should also be extended to women.

In March 1867, the Kansas legislature submitted two separate constitutional amendments to the voters of the state. One was designed to allow black males to vote; the other would give the vote to women. The November election of 1867 would tell whether Kansas voters wanted blacks, women, or both to be *enfranchised* (granted the right to vote).

The Kansas campaign marked the first time that the question of *universal suffrage* (voting by all citizens) would be decided by the people. No other state had universal suffrage at the time. Kansas was again the focus of national attention.

At first the constitutional amendments seemed popular in the state. By early summer it was clear that support from the Republican party had become lukewarm. Although the two proposals had been sponsored by Republicans in the legislature, the party remained officially neutral during the campaign. One faction of the party became publicly hostile to the woman suffrage amendment. Members of that faction argued that party support for woman suffrage would lead to defeat of black suffrage.

Lacking official Republican support, those in Kansas who favored both proposals sought help elsewhere. Their search led to abolitionist leaders in the East, whose words still carried weight with many who had fought against slavery during the time of Bleeding Kansas. The universal suffrage forces in Kansas were soon disappointed. Support they expected from eastern abolitionists did not come. Many of the abolitionists feared that a link to woman suffrage would be a political burden for their program of freedmen's rights.

Suffrage forces in Kansas turned next to a group in the East called the Equal Rights Association. Members of this group, mostly women who were former abolitionists, were dedicated to universal suffrage. These suffragists viewed Kansas as a testing ground for their goal. Several of the group's leaders accepted the invitation to come to Kansas and canvass the state for the two proposed amendments. One of those who came to Kansas, expecting that state would vote for woman suffrage just as it had voted against slavery, was Susan B. Anthony.

Susan was born in 1820 near Adams, Massachusetts. Her Quaker family lived comfortably on a farm. Hard work and skill were valued highly during Susan's upbringing.

When Susan was two years old her enterprising father built a cotton factory. As a child Susan often observed the millworkers doing their jobs. "If Sally Ann knows more about weaving than Elijah," said young Susan to her father, "then why don't you make her overseer?" Her father replied that it would never do to have a woman overseer in the mill. This answer did not satisfy Susan. She was puzzled that skilled women were never put in charge.

At age 15, Susan became a teacher. In her first teaching job she replaced a man who had been discharged for doing a poor job. It disturbed Susan that she was paid only one-fourth the salary the male teacher had received.

One summer during her teaching career Susan studied algebra, something unusual for a woman at the time. Proud of her knowledge, she stopped over for a visit with her sister, Guelma, and brother-in-law, Aaron. Eagerly she told them of her new accomplishment. Later, at dinner, Susan served biscuits she had baked. Aaron remarked, "I'd rather see a woman make biscuits like these than solve the knottiest problem in algebra." "There is no reason," Susan replied, "why we should not be able to do both."

In 1848 Susan read newspaper accounts of the first women's rights convention held in Seneca Falls, New York. The women assembled there proclaimed themselves men's equals. They also protested against all forms of discrimination against women. What most captured Susan's attention was a call for woman suffrage from Elizabeth Cady Stanton, one of the delegates to the Seneca Falls Convention.

Susan had never thought much about the inferior legal status of women. Now, for the first time, she began to ponder restrictions placed upon members of her sex. Married women were not allowed to own property in their own names. Their earnings and inheritance were turned over to their husbands. If their marriages broke up, women had no right to the joint guardianship of their children. Women were also excluded from colleges. Susan came to regard the vote for women as the best way to remove these restrictions.

In 1850 Susan B. Anthony met Elizabeth Cady Stanton, the out-spoken advocate of woman suffrage at Seneca Falls. While walking home together from an antislavery meeting one night, the two women discussed abolition and women's rights. A lifelong friendship began that evening. Mrs. Stanton's clear thinking had instant appeal for Miss Anthony. This mother of three boys offered Susan conversation she had never had before with another woman. They grew very close, rebelling as they did against the belief that women were naturally sheltered from want and care by men.

Anthony frequently visited her friend's home in Seneca Falls. By being there she enabled Stanton to write articles and speeches in favor of women's rights. Susan would prepare meals for the boys, wash their laundry, discipline them, and change the baby's diapers. At night, when the children were asleep, the women discussed the issues of the day. As a result of their discussions, both women became founders and leaders of the Equal Rights Association. From its beginning this group proposed that the movements for black suffrage and woman suffrage be united in a single demand for universal suffrage.

By 1858 the whole country was tense over the slavery issue. Susan Anthony had been put in charge of the American Antislavery Society for the state of New York. For ten dollars a week she arranged meetings, displayed posters, and planned tours for speakers.

Just as she began her antislavery work a heavily veiled woman came to Susan for help one night in Albany, New York. The woman told a tragic story. She was married to Dr. Charles A. Phelps, a Massachusetts senator, and was mother of their three children. When she confronted her husband with evidence that he had been unfaithful, he had her committed to an insane asylum. After a year and a half her brother arranged for her to be temporarily released. Dr. Phelps agreed to allow the children to visit their mother for a few weeks. After the time was up, Massachusetts authorities were about to separate Mrs. Phelps again from her children. With one of her children, she fled across the state line to Susan.

Susan decided to hide the woman and her 13-year-old daughter. Wearing disguises they took the train with Susan to New York City on Christmas Day. Because they weren't accompanied by a gentleman, they were refused a hotel room. Susan then walked them through the snow and slush to a boardinghouse run by a woman she knew. The woman refused them. She feared her boarders would leave if she harbored a runaway wife. Eventually Susan persuaded a hotel clerk to give them a room without heat for the night. The following day one of Susan's friends agreed to take the runaways into her home.

When Susan returned to Albany, she was threatened with arrest. She had broken the law by depriving a father of his child. Despite the threat Miss Anthony refused to reveal Mrs. Phelps' hiding place.

William Lloyd Garrison, the well-known abolitionist, urged Susan Anthony not to injure the reputation of the antislavery cause by hiding a fugitive wife. In a letter, Garrison put this question to Anthony, "Don't you know that the law of Massachusetts gives the father the entire guardianship and control of the children?" Susan responded:

> Yes, I know it. Does not the law of the United States give the slaveholder the ownership of the slave? And don't you break it every time you help a slave to Canada? Well, the law which gives the father sole ownership of the children is just as wicked and I'll break it just as quickly. You would die before you would deliver a slave to his master, and I will die before I will give up that child to its father.

Dr. Phelps managed to seize his child on her way to Sunday School.

With the outbreak of the Civil War, the momentum of the first decade of the women's rights movement came to a sudden halt. Women devoted their efforts to winning the war. With their husbands and sons off to battle, many women carried on alone in the home, on the farm, and in business. Some sewed and knitted for soldiers. During the war years, Susan urged women to think about more than socks and bandages. She wanted them to help mold public opinion in favor of woman suffrage.

The suffragists' cause was bolstered by women who made outstanding contributions to the Union war effort. Anna E. Carroll, for example, persuaded President Lincoln to abandon a planned military campaign down the Mississippi River in favor of her own plan of attack down the Tennessee River. Her plan succeeded in cutting the Confederacy in two. Dorothea Dix, as government superintendent of nurses, improved hospital care for wounded soldiers. On the battlefields Clara Barton established the forerunner of the American Red Cross. In Susan's opinion, women had earned their right to vote.

During the war abolitionists asked women to be patient. It was "the Negro hour" they were told. They must step aside and wait their turn. Once the conflict was settled the course of woman suffrage would be revived. That promise led Susan to expect great strides for women's rights during Reconstruction.

Her attention naturally turned to Kansas in 1867 where she envisioned a joint triumph for black and woman suffrage. Kansas could prove the two compatible. With Elizabeth Cady Stanton, she left for Lawrence, Kansas. They were determined to stand firmly behind suffrage for both blacks and women.

When Anthony and Stanton arrived in Kansas in early September, they found the prosuffrage forces there demoralized. As a result of opposition from Republicans the campaign for the suffrage amendments had all but collapsed. Funds were low and election day was closing in.

Susan and Elizabeth did everything they could to revive the campaign. On a tour of the state they traveled in an open carriage from village to town, speaking at least once a day. These upper-class eastern women were unaccustomed to the rugged frontier conditions in Kansas. They dined on the likes of "bacon floating in grease, coffee without milk, . . . and bread or hot biscuit, green with soda." Often they slept with bedbugs, pigs, or mice.

Before meeting her, many thought Susan would be a meddlesome, sour old maid. They discovered she was not the person they had been led to expect. On the lecture platform she wore a gray silk dress with a soft, white lace collar. Her hair was smoothed back and twisted neatly into a tight knot. Everything about her indicated refinement and sincerity. Most of her audience felt this. She spoke to them as equals. Though usually serious, even stern, her face lighted up with a friendly smile. Gradually, Susan won over a following.

Her enemies, however, argued fiercely against woman suffrage. They offered five major reasons to oppose the vote for Kansas women:

1. God had given different spheres of activity to men and women. It was His wish that both remain in their appointed places.
2. Women were adequately represented by men already.
3. Women were unable to perform the physical duties of citizens such as bearing arms or doing heavy labor and thus could not defend the rights of citizenship.
4. Women who took part in politics would neglect their household duties and destroy the harmony of home and family.
5. Feminine purity and delicacy would be destroyed if women became active in politics.

By the final stage of the campaign the suffragists had grown desperate for money. Their funds were all spent, and they had another month to go. At this point they received an unexpected offer of aid.

In early October a telegram arrived for Susan Anthony from a Democrat in Omaha named George Francis Train. He offered to come to Kansas at his own expense and help in the campaign to win the vote for women. Train was famous as a world traveler and successful businessman. He made a huge fortune as a financier, builder of clipper ships, and railroad promoter. At the time of the Kansas campaign, he was beginning to promote himself for the presidency of the United States. With the eyes of the nation upon Kansas, Train shrewdly considered the suffrage campaign a good source of publicity.

George Francis Train was a controversial figure. Though brilliant and entertaining, he was known nationally as a *Copperhead* (Southern sympathizer during the Civil War). He was a champion of women's rights, but he was an opponent of rights for blacks. His views were at odds with the Equal Rights Association tradition of support for both black and woman suffrage.

Train feared political power for freedmen. That fear was at the root of his support for woman suffrage. He regarded female suffrage as a way to offset blacks' votes. If black men voted, he reasoned, the political supremacy of whites could be maintained by giving the vote to women.

George Train publicly expressed his view on the two Kansas amendments:

> Black men are emancipated, white women are still enslaved. Black slaves once, legally, had no power. Their masters were supreme. Now black freemen have all power except the ballot. Give them that, . . . and what chance has woman after? Ignorance will not vote for intelligence, vice will not vote for virtue, ugliness will not vote for beauty.

It was well known that Train considered the whole black race as inferior and incapable of improvement. To those who intended to vote for black suffrage and against woman suffrage he said:

> Not satisfied with having your mother, your wife, your sisters, your daughters the equals politically of the negro—by giving him a vote and refusing it to women, you wish to place your family politically still lower in the scale of citizenship and humanity. . . . Women first, and negro last, is my programme.

Train could put on the best show to be found on the Kansas prairies. A flamboyant figure, he drew large crowds. His bearing suggested the dapper old school gentleman. He never appeared before an audience without a change, shave, and cologne rinse. While speaking, he appeared always in lavender kid gloves, black pants, closely buttoned blue coat with brass buttons, and patent leather boots. Age 35, tall, handsome, and in vigorous health, he charmed his audiences.

Train's offer of help posed a difficult decision for Anthony. He could organize Democratic voters in support of woman suffrage. He could persuade those opposed to black suffrage to take up the women's cause. Most tempting, he offered money to finance the bankrupt campaign for a cross-country lecture tour and a women's rights journal, both cherished dreams for Susan.

If Susan accepted George's offer she would be going against the wishes of respected friends. Lucy Stone, another famed suffragist, for example, threatened to resign from the Equal Rights Association if

Train's offers were accepted. Anthony also knew that her abolitionist allies would be enraged by Train's racism.

With 20 days remaining in the campaign, Anthony wired Train to come to Kansas and stump the state. He accompanied Susan on a speaking tour and aroused their audiences with his wit, charm, and exuberance. He also contributed more than $3,000.

On the first Tuesday of November Kansas voters made their decision. Black suffrage was defeated by a vote of 19,420 to 10,483. Woman suffrage also went down to defeat, 19,857 votes to 9,070. Train's help had not been decisive.

Anthony was disappointed with the results, but she took heart that one of every three male voters in Kansas favored woman suffrage. She looked forward to her upcoming lecture tour with Train and to publishing the new journal.

The year after the Kansas campaign the Fifteenth Amendment to the U.S. Constitution was ratified. One of three Reconstruction amendments, it granted the right to vote to black men. Women were still denied the vote.

In 1906 Susan B. Anthony died. By that year only four states had granted the vote to women: Wyoming, Utah, Colorado, and Idaho. A few years earlier Susan had been asked whether she believed that all women in the United States would ever be able to vote. She said, "It will come, but I shall not see it. It is inevitable. We can no more deny forever the right of self-government to one half our people than we could keep the Negro forever in bondage."

Fourteen years after her death, on August 26, 1920, women were enfranchised throughout the United States by the Nineteenth Amendment.

The major sources for this story were:

Dubois, Ellen C. "A New Life: The Development of an American Woman Suffrage Movement, 1860 1869." Ph.D. dissertation, Northwestern University, 1975.

Lutz, Alma. *Susan B. Anthony*. Boston: Beacon Press, 1959.

Madsen, Sandra A. "The 1867 Campaign for Woman Suffrage in Kansas: A Study in Rhetorical Situation." Ph.D. dissertation, University of Kansas, 1975.

Stanton, Elizabeth C., Anthony, Susan B., and Gage, Matilda, J., eds. *History of Women Suffrage*. Vol. 2, *1861 1876*. New York: Fowler and Wells, 1882.

ACTIVITIES FOR "PIONEER SUFFRAGIST"

Answer all questions on a separate sheet of paper.

Historical Understanding

Answer briefly:

1. What effect did popular sovereignty have upon the Missouri Compromise?
2. Why was Kansas referred to as Bleeding Kansas?
3. Define the following: abolitionist, freedmen, suffragist, universal suffrage, Copperhead.
4. During Reconstruction, what was the major political goal of former abolitionists?
5. Why did many Republicans and former abolitionists withhold their support for woman suffrage after the Civil War?
6. What important event occurred in 1848 at Seneca Falls, New York?
7. What were two major accomplishments of American women during the Civil War?
8. What changes were made to the U.S. Constitution by the Fifteenth and Nineteenth Amendments?

Reviewing the Facts of the Case

Answer briefly:

1. What two changes were proposed for the Kansas Constitution in 1867?
2. What was the Equal Rights Association and what position did it take on the issue of suffrage?
3. What did Miss Anthony do when Mrs. Phelps came to her in Albany for help?

4. Describe the offer Susan B. Anthony received from George Francis Train.

5. Why did Lucy Stone and former abolitionists dislike George Francis Train?

Analyzing Ethical Issues

There are several incidents in this story in which people made decisions involving equality (a value concerning whether people should be treated in the same way.) Sometimes the value of equality came into conflict with one of the following values:

PROPERTY: A value concerning what people should be allowed to own and how they should be allowed to use it.

AUTHORITY: A value concerning what people, customs, or rules should be obeyed and the consequences for disobedience.

Identify one incident from the story in which equality conflicts with one of these values. Indicate which other value was involved and which value was chosen, as illustrated by this example:

INCIDENT	VALUE IN CONFLICT WITH EQUALITY	VALUE CHOSEN
Kansas settlers exercising "popular sovereignty" in 1850s	*Property*	*Equality*

Expressing Your Reasoning

1. Should Susan Anthony have accepted George Francis Train's offer of help? Why or why not?

2. A familiar saying suggests that we should "never look a gift horse in the mouth." Elizabeth Cady Stanton agreed with Susan B. Anthony's decision to accept Train's offer. In defense of that decision Stanton wrote to the treasurer of the Equal Rights Association: "If the devil steps forward to help, I say good fellow come on!" For each situation below decide whether or not you think the offer ought to be accepted and state a reason for your position.

a. A slum landlord offers a contribution to build a school for nurses.
b. A known drug dealer offers to pay college tuition for an impoverished student.
c. A voter is offered $25 to vote for a candidate he was already planning to vote for.
d. A child is offered a pair of ice skates purchased from someone who had stolen them.
e. A player cut from his football team offers team plays to the opposing team before the game.

Some people believe the ends justify the means. Can you think of a means that would be wrong even if it accomplished a good end? Explain.

3. Those in Kansas who campaigned against woman suffrage offered five reasons to oppose the vote for women:
    a. God had given different spheres of activity to men and women. It was His wish that both remain in their appointed places.
    b. Women were adequately represented by men already.
    c. Women were unable to perform the physical duties of citizens, such as bearing arms or doing heavy labor, and thus could not defend the rights of citizenship.
    d. Women who took part in politics would neglect their household duties and destroy the harmony of home and family.
    e. Feminine purity and delicacy would be destroyed if women became active in politics.

Write a few paragraphs explaining what you think would be the best challenge to each of the arguments above.

4. During the Kansas campaign, Susan's opponents argued that it would be wrong to grant the vote to women. They claimed both sexes had "different spheres of activity" and should "remain in their appointed places." For the following situations decide whether or not you think equal consideration should be given to males and females. State a reason for your opinions.
    a. Serve in military combat.
    b. Do household chores such as dishwashing, laundry, cooking, or plumbing repairs.
    c. Receive time off from a job to care for a newborn infant.
    d. Participate in high school athletics.
    e. Take a different last name after marriage.

5. *Seeking Additional Information.* In making decisions about such
   questions as those above, we often feel we need more information
   before we are satisfied with our judgment. Choose one of the
   above questions about which you would like more information
   than is presented in the story. What additional information would
   you like? Why would that information help you make a more
   satisfactory decision?

The Beast and The "Bagger"

RECONSTRUCTION IN LOUISIANA

(*State Historical Society of Wisconsin*)

Benjamin F. Butler

The Civil War came quickly to Louisiana. In April 1862, federal gunboats commanded by David Farragut captured New Orleans for the North. The Stars and Stripes were raised over the federal mint, and the people awaited the arrival of General Benjamin Butler. He was to have command of the city.

Before Butler arrived, a Southerner named Mumford ripped the Union flag from its pole at the mint. When Butler arrived, he had Mumford publicly hanged in front of the mint. Butler was determined to keep order in the war-troubled city. When some of his soldiers stole goods from a private home, he had them hanged as well.

Butler said: "New Orleans is a conquered city . . . and by the law of nations lies subject to the will of the conqueror." To the people of New Orleans he became known as Beast Butler.

The firm hand of the Beast was felt throughout the city. Newspapers that printed articles critical of him were shut down. He insisted that ministers offer prayers for President Lincoln and not honor the Confederacy in their church services. Those who refused to obey had their churches closed. One of his most controversial actions was called the Woman's Order. Many of the women of New Orleans showed their disgust of federal troops by spitting at them and insulting them in other ways. Butler ordered that such women be treated as streetwalkers to be arrested or fined. People were outraged that women should be treated that way. Nonetheless, the order seemed to work, for Butler reported that the "she-rebels" had stopped their insults.

In July 1862, Congress passed a law saying that the property of rebels could be seized and used by the government. Butler ordered all citizens to register the property they owned and to declare whether they were loyal to the United States. Those who took the loyalty oath would not lose their property. A minister urged Butler not to enforce the taking of the oath because many people would be forced to lie to protect their property. Butler did not accept the advice. Eventually over 60,000 people took the oath, while about 4,000 registered as enemies of the United States. It was said that many who were still loyal to the Confederacy falsely proclaimed their loyalty to the Union.

While it was important to the North to win the war militarily, it was also important to bring conquered rebel states back into the Union. The political wounds of war had to be healed. Even as the war continued, politicians argued about how the South should be treated after the war.

A group of men in Congress known as the Radical Republicans wanted the defeated Southern states to be treated harshly for leaving the Union. President Lincoln preferred to be more lenient and forgiving. Plans for how the South should be treated were known as Reconstruction plans. Legally it was not clear whether the president or Congress should be in charge of Reconstruction. Lincoln tried to take charge.

Late in 1863, as the war continued, Lincoln said that all Southerners, except certain officers and officials of the Confederacy, would be pardoned for leaving the Union if they took a loyalty oath. Then, when the number of people having taken the oath equaled 10 percent of a state's voting population in the 1860 election, they could elect representatives to create a new state government. The new government would have to accept the permanent abolition of slavery. If these conditions were met, the president would recognize the government as legal. Congress, however, would have the authority to decide if representatives from the state should be allowed to take their seats in Washington.

Because New Orleans and about one-half of Louisiana were controlled by federal troops, the state was to be a testing ground for Lincoln's Reconstruction plan. General Nathaniel Banks had replaced Butler and, early in 1863, Lincoln urged him to help establish a new state government.

Banks pushed hard for voter registration. For many years before the war, there had been a large, nonslave black population in New Orleans. Among this group were well-educated property owners, but, because of their color, they had never been allowed to vote. A group of these people sent a petition to Banks. In it they said they had always been peaceful, taxpaying people and that they were loyal to the Union and believed they had the right to vote. Banks ignored their request and declared that only 21-year-old white males who took the loyalty oath could vote.

Banks insisted that all eligible voters should vote. People who wanted to be neutral were angered, but Banks said: "Indifference will be treated as a crime." A newspaper quoted his policy as: "Vote, fight, or leave!" In spite of his statements, Banks did not enforce his threats to punish nonvoters.

More than 10 percent of the eligible voters signed the loyalty oath, and the election was held in February 1864. Two months later representatives met to draw up a new state constitution.

Banks and Lincoln were pleased with the progress, and Lincoln recognized the newly elected state officials as legal. Many Louisianans refused to accept the new government. They said that much of the state was still in Confederate hands, and there was a Confederate state capital at Shreveport. Furthermore, the military, they believed, had forced the new government on them.

Some blacks and white Radical Republicans were displeased with the new government, because it did not permit blacks to vote. In a letter to the new governor of Louisiana, Lincoln said: "I barely suggest for your private consideration whether some of the colored people may not be let in, as for instance the very intelligent and especially those who have fought gallantly in our ranks." Although Lincoln's suggestion may seem mild, almost timid, allowing any blacks to vote would have been a dramatic step for any Southern state and most Northern ones as well. The new state government refused to allow blacks to vote.

Controversy over the new state government continued, but war-torn Louisiana faced economic and social problems as well as political ones. Cutting through all of the problems was racial tension. For years, slavery had defined the position of most blacks in Louisiana. For example, in 1830 a law made it illegal to teach slaves to read or write. Then, almost overnight, tens of thousands of slaves, most of whom were illiterate, were freed. Many came to New Orleans and other cities, while others remained in rural areas. Some were hired to work on plantations, but wages were low. Also, for many blacks, working on plantations was like returning to slavery. For ex-slaves in the cities, only a few jobs were available.

For a time, Louisiana, like some other Southern states, passed laws regulating the behavior of black people. In November 1865, Louisiana passed the Vagrant Law. According to this law, anyone who wandered about without a job could be arrested. Once arrested, the person could be hired out to work on plantations or to labor on public works, such as repairing the levees that held back flood waters. Technically, the law applied to both whites and blacks. Many Northerners, however, suspected that such laws were a veiled attempt to reinstate slavery.

Not all white Louisianans opposed black rights. Among this group of people were some white Radical Republicans. Many of the Radical Republicans in Louisiana had been born in the North and were called *carpetbaggers* by native white Louisianans. Supposedly, these Northerners had packed their belongings in bags made of carpet material and hurried South to make money by meddling in political affairs. Louisiana's Radical Republicans disagreed about some black rights, but all agreed that blacks should be allowed to vote. Of course, if given the vote, it was likely that blacks would support the Republicans.

The Congress had refused to seat Louisiana representatives elected under the 1864 constitution, largely because blacks were not allowed to vote. Therefore, Louisiana was not officially back in the Union. After Lincoln's death, President Andrew Johnson urged the white Democrats, then in control of Louisiana's government, to allow blacks who paid taxes and who could read the Constitution to vote. If that were done, Johnson believed Congress would accept Louisiana into the Union. However, the Democrats would not go along with the idea. They doubted that a majority of Louisiana whites would support black voting. Blacks were allowed to vote in only a few Northern states. Many Louisiana whites thought it was unfair to force the South to do something not required in the North.

In early 1866, the Radical Republicans in Louisiana called a new constitutional convention. They believed they could create a constitution acceptable to Congress, and, with federal support, take control of the state government. The convention met in New Orleans; the outcome was a calamity. On July 30, a group of blacks, who were marching to attend the convention, got into a battle with a group of hostile whites. In the fighting, over thirty blacks were killed and at least one hundred were wounded. The police force was involved in the gunbattle against the blacks.

News of the killings in New Orleans spread quickly through the North. More and more people felt that such violence meant the federal government should adopt harsher Reconstruction measures. This feeling helped the Radical Republicans in the national elections of 1866. The Radical Republicans now controlled Congress and took over Reconstruction.

Early in 1867, Congress passed a number of laws governing Reconstruction. In accordance with these laws, the South was divided into five military districts, each commanded by a Union officer. No state would be readmitted to the Union unless it created a new constitution guaranteeing blacks the right to vote. Representatives to the new constitutional conventions had to be elected by both blacks and whites. In addition, those who had held civil offices in the

Confederacy, or had been officers of the Confederate army, were not allowed to vote.

General Philip Sheridan was appointed military commander of the district that included Louisiana. His use of power quickly angered many white Louisianans. For example, he ordered a reorganization of the New Orleans police force, which had been involved in the 1866 riot, so that one-half of its membership would be composed of former Union soldiers. Also, Sheridan would not enforce the segregation policy that had operated for many years on New Orleans' streetcars. Blacks had been only allowed to ride on special "star" cars. When some blacks tried to ride on white-only cars, the owners of the company asked Sheridan to enforce segregation. Sheridan refused the owner's request. The general also organized voter registration drives, and many more blacks than whites registered. This was not surprising because there were more blacks than whites in the state. Many white Louisianans were fearful of what would happen if blacks controlled the government. They were especially fearful of social integration, which they believed would force the races together. Concern increased when a black newspaper editor wrote: "We want to ride in any conveyance, to travel on steamboats, eat in any steamboat, dine at any restaurant, or educate our children at any school."

Some whites were frightened to the extreme. According to one opinion, furious blacks were going to rewrite the history of the state "in letters of blood, for they daily and openly threaten arson, rape, murder, rebellion, civil war, and the extermination of the whites." It is doubtful that blacks ever made such threats. It was, however, certain that many whites were afraid of what black political power would bring.

As directed by Congress, a new state constitution was written guaranteeing blacks the right to vote. Statewide elections, under military supervision, were held, and Henry Clay Warmouth, a white man, was elected governor. The Radical Republicans were now in control of Louisiana, and the state was readmitted to the Union in June of 1868.

Warmouth was regarded as a carpetbagger. Born in Illinois, he served in the Union army and later became involved in Louisiana politics.

The young governor, aged 26, had his hands full. Most white Louisianans did not support the Radical Republicans. They looked with disdain at the new state government and its legislature that was about one-half black.

To oppose the Radical Republicans, many whites looked to the Democratic party, and some joined secret organizations. These organizations were dedicated to the return of white control of Louisiana. Secret meetings, codes, oaths, and handshakes were devised so that the groups could keep their operations a mystery to outsiders. At the time, the best known of these organizations was the Knights of the White Camelia. Governor Warmouth said he had received a death threat from the Ku Klux Klan, another secret white group.

One of the purposes of the secret groups was to prevent blacks from voting for Republicans. Often physical violence was used or threatened. As the presidential election of 1868 approached, there were many terrible battles between blacks and whites throughout the state. There was virtually no law and order in Louisiana. Fears of even greater violence led Warmouth and other Republicans to urge blacks not to vote in the coming election.

The threats and violence seemed to work. One member of the Knights of the White Camelia wrote: "The true white people of New Orleans are strong and confident of . . . complete success, not only in November, but forever after." At that time there was no secret ballot, and on election day one supervisor of registration said: "I am fully convinced that no man could have voted any other than the Democratic ticket and not been killed inside of twenty-four hours."

The Democrats obtained a huge majority of the state's votes. They did not win nationally, however, and General Ulysses Grant, a Republican and Union war hero, became president.

State officials had not been up for election in the November voting, but the results were a warning. Warmouth believed he and the Republicans could not remain in power unless they could prevent future elections from being decided by threats and terror. Warmouth's supporters in the legislature passed a law creating the Returning Board. This board, controlled by the governor, had the power to count election returns and throw out votes if they thought voters in an area had been frightened or terrorized in some way. Critics of Warmouth were disgusted. There was no legal way to prevent the board from simply throwing out Democratic votes in future elections.

Warmouth and the Republican-controlled legislature received much criticism. Like many other Southern Reconstruction governments,

Louisiana's was plagued by corruption. Legislators commonly took bribes to pass laws that helped particular people or businesses. Warmouth was often unfairly accused of corruption, but he did make money while in office. For example, he arranged for all of the state's printing business to be done by a company of which he was a major stockholder.

In one instance, the state senate was deadlocked by a vote of 17 to 17 in trying to decide on a new lieutenant governor. Warmouth offered one of the white senators a bribe of $15,000 plus $20,000 in state bonds if the senator would vote for Warmouth's candidate, a well-known black man named Pinchback. The senator agreed. The money was to be placed in a metal box and held by a banker until after the final vote. The vote was held and Pinchback won 18 to 16. When the senator picked up the metal box there was no money to be found.

Warmouth agreed that bribery was widespread but emphasized that there was no state law against bribery at that time. At one point Warmouth supposedly said: "I don't pretend to be honest. . . . I only pretend to be as honest as anybody in politics, and more so than those fellows who are opposing me now."

Warmouth gradually lost the support of the Radical Republicans. Like most white Louisianans of the time, he was not in favor of black social equality. He believed blacks should vote, and their support had helped him win elections, but he did not support other rights for blacks. When the legislature passed a law making it a crime to deny blacks equal service on steamboats, in restaurants, hotels, and other public places, Warmouth vetoed it. He said the law should not force the races to be together: "It ought to be carefully borne in mind that we can not hope by legislation to control questions of personal association." He said that such laws would create more racial tension and have bad long-term effects.

The governor recognized that he was losing black and other Republican support and did not run for the office again. He remained in Louisiana, however, and witnessed the confusion and tragedy of the remaining years of Reconstruction in Louisiana.

The battle for political control of Louisiana continued. Federal troops were often used to support Radical Republican governments. Racial tension and bloody confrontations were all too common. After Rutherford Hayes became president in 1876, federal troops were withdrawn from the South and Reconstruction officially ended. In Louisiana, Radical Republican rule had ended forever, and the Democratic party became the major political power.

The major sources for this story were:

Ficklen, John R. *History of Reconstruction in Louisiana.* Baltimore: Johns Hopkins Press, 1910.

Harris, Francis B. "Henry Clay Warmouth, Reconstruction Governor of Louisiana." *The Louisiana Historical Quarterly,* April 1947, pp. 523–653.

Taylor, Joe G. *Louisiana Reconstructed.* Baton Rouge: Louisiana State University Press, 1974.

ACTIVITIES FOR "THE BEAST AND THE 'BAGGER'"

Answer all questions on a separate sheet of paper.

Historical Understanding

Answer briefly:

1. In what ways did Lincoln's plan for Reconstruction differ from the plan of the Radical Republicans?

2. What was a carpetbagger?

3. What were two causes of racial tension between blacks and whites after the Civil War?

4. Describe three ways the federal government involved itself in Louisiana politics.

Reviewing the Facts of the Case

Answer briefly:

1. Who was General Butler? Why was he known as the Beast?

2. Who was General Banks? What did New Orleans blacks ask of him? How did he respond?

3. What was the Vagrant Law? Why was it passed?

4. Who was General Sheridan? Why was he unpopular among many Louisiana whites?

5. What was the Returning Board?

6. Who was Henry Warmouth? Why did he gradually lose black and Republican support?

7. What was the Knights of the White Camelia? Why was it created?

Analyzing Ethical Issues

There are a number of incidents in this story involving the following values:

AUTHORITY: a value concerning what rules or people should be obeyed and the consequences for disobedience.

EQUALITY: a value concerning whether people should be treated in the same way.

LIBERTY: a value concerning what freedoms people should have and the limits that may be justifiably placed on them.

LIFE: a value concerning when, if ever, it is justifiable to threaten or take the life of another.

PROMISE-KEEPING: a value concerning the nature of duties that arise when promises are made.

For each of the values above—authority, equality, liberty, life, promise-keeping—write a sentence describing an incident from the story involving that value, as illustrated by this example:

Life: *Warmouth claimed that his life had been threatened by the Ku Klux Klan.*

Expressing Your Reasoning

1. The question of who should be allowed to vote was raised constantly during the Reconstruction era. At different times the following categories of people were either allowed or denied the vote. (At that time, there was no significant consideration of giving the vote to women or people under the age of 21.) During Reconstruction, should any of the following categories of people have been denied the vote? Explain your reasoning for each group.

    a. Black men who could not read or write.

    b. White men who could not read or write.

    c. Black men who did not own property or pay taxes.

    d. White men who did not own property or pay taxes.

    e. White men who were officers or officials in the Confederate goverment.

    f. Men who refused to take an oath of loyalty to the United States.

2. When the legislature passed a law making it a crime to deny blacks equal access to restaurants, hotels, and transportation facilities, Warmouth vetoed the law. He said that the government should not try to regulate the way people associate with one another. Do you agree with Warmouth? Why or why not?

3. A minister asked Butler not to enforce the loyalty oath because it would force them to lie to save their property. Would it be wrong for a person falsely to claim loyalty to save his or her property? Why or why not? Write a paragraph expressing your opinion.

4. *Seeking Additional Information.* In making decisions about such questions as those above, we often feel we need more information before we are satisfied with our judgments. Choose one of the above questions about which you would like more information than is presented in the story. What additional information would you like? Why would the information help you make a more satisfactory decision?